Taxcafe.co.uk Tax Guides

Property Capital Gains Tax

How to Pay the Absolute Minimum CGT on Rental Properties & Second Homes

By Carl Bayley BSc ACA

&

Nick Braun PhD

Important Legal Notices:

Taxcafe®
Tax Guide - "Property Capital Gains Tax"

Published by:
Taxcafe UK Limited
67 Milton Road
Kirkcaldy KY1 1TL
Tel: (0044) 01592 560081
Email: team@taxcafe.co.uk

ISBN 978-1-907302-54-1

Fourth edition, April 2012

Trademarks
Taxcafe® is a registered trademark of Taxcafe UK Limited. All other trademarks, names and logos in this tax guide may be trademarks of their respective owners.

Disclaimer
Before reading or relying on the content of this tax guide please read carefully the disclaimer.

Disclaimer

1. This guide is intended as **general guidance** only and does NOT constitute accountancy, tax, investment or other professional advice.

2. The authors and Taxcafe UK Limited make no representations or warranties with respect to the accuracy or completeness of this publication and cannot accept any responsibility or liability for any loss or risk, personal or otherwise, which may arise, directly or indirectly, from reliance on information contained in this publication.

3. Please note that tax legislation, the law and practices by Government and regulatory authorities (e.g. HM Revenue & Customs) are constantly changing. We therefore recommend that for accountancy, tax, investment or other professional advice, you consult a suitably qualified accountant, tax specialist, independent financial adviser, or other professional adviser.

4. Please also note that your personal circumstances may vary from the general examples given in this guide and your professional adviser will be able to give specific advice based on your personal circumstances.

5. This guide covers UK taxation only and any references to 'tax' or 'taxation', unless the contrary is expressly stated, refer to UK taxation only. Please note that references to the 'UK' do not include the Channel Islands or the Isle of Man. Foreign tax implications are beyond the scope of this guide.

6. All persons described in the examples in this guide are entirely fictional. Any similarities to actual persons, living or dead, or to fictional characters created by any other author, are entirely coincidental.

About the Authors & Taxcafe

Carl Bayley is the author of a series of Taxcafe guides designed specifically for the layman. Carl's particular speciality is his ability to take the weird, complex and inexplicable world of taxation and set it out in the kind of clear, straightforward language that taxpayers themselves can understand. As he often says himself, "my job is to translate tax into English".

In addition to being a recognised author, Carl has often spoken on taxation on radio and television, including the Jeremy Vine Show on BBC Radio 2.

A chartered accountant by training, Carl is also a member of the governing Council of the Institute of Chartered Accountants in England and Wales.

Nick Braun founded Taxcafe.co.uk in 1999, along with his partner, Aileen Smith. As the driving force behind the company, their aim is to provide affordable plain-English tax information for private individuals and investors, business owners, IFAs and accountants.

Since then Taxcafe has become one of the best-known tax publishers in the UK and has won several business awards.

Nick has been involved in the tax publishing world since 1989 as a writer, editor and publisher. He holds a doctorate in economics from the University of Glasgow, where he was awarded the prestigious William Glen Scholarship and later became a Research Fellow. Prior to that, he graduated with distinction from the University of South Africa, the country's oldest university, earning the highest results in economics in the university's history.

Contents

Chapter 1

Introduction

In the 2010 'emergency Budget' the new Chancellor of the Exchequer, George Osborne, announced some important changes to capital gains tax.

The current rules apply to all disposals that take place after 22nd June 2010. It doesn't matter whether you bought your property before or after this date.

As a result of these changes, capital gains tax has become more costly and more complicated.

The flat 18% capital gains tax rate, which used to apply to everyone, was scrapped and replaced with two tax rates:

- 18% for basic-rate taxpayers
- 28% for higher-rate taxpayers

What this change means is the amount of capital gains tax you currently pay depends on how much *income* you have earned during the tax year.

The amount of tax you pay also depends upon the size of your capital gains. Your capital gains are added to your income, so even someone with no income but large capital gains could end up paying tax at 28% on some of their gains.

In Chapter 10 we will show you how to reduce your taxable income so that your capital gains are taxed at just 18%.

Inflation Protection

When the Chancellor of the Exchequer introduced the higher 28% tax rate he did not bring back indexation relief or taper relief to protect long-term investors from the ravages of inflation. So someone who has owned a property for one year will pay tax at the same rate as someone who has owned a property for 20 years.

This means that the new 28% tax rate is potentially higher than it was under even the old pre-2008 tax regime. Under those rules, capital gains were taxed at up to 40% but, thanks to taper relief, the effective rate for long-term investors who held on to assets for more than 10 years was just 24%.

The Annual CGT Exemption

Back in 2010 there was a rumour going around that the annual capital gains tax exemption would be drastically reduced.

But in the June 2010 emergency Budget the Chancellor of the Exchequer promised that this tax relief, instead of being reduced, "will continue to rise with inflation in future years".

Unfortunately, this promise has now been broken. The annual CGT exemption was £10,600 for the 2011/12 tax year. It has been frozen at £10,600 for the 2012/13 tax year, commencing on 6th April 2012. So no inflation uplift this year.

In Chapter 12 we will show you how to obtain extra tax savings by making better use of your annual CGT exemption.

Furnished Holiday Lets

You have to pass a number of tests to qualify for furnished holiday let tax treatment but, for those that do, it's the tax equivalent of winning the lottery.

Owners of furnished holiday lets enjoy a host of special income tax and capital gains tax concessions.

The previous Labour government tried to kill these off ahead of the last general election but ran out of time. To the delight of many owners of holiday cottages and apartments, the Conservatives won a last-minute stay of execution.

As a result, the favourable furnished holiday letting tax regime continues to exist and applies to properties both in the UK and elsewhere in the European Economic Area (EEA).

That's the good news. The bad news is the qualifying criteria have been tightened and some changes have been made to the tax concessions available.

In Chapters 20 and 21 we explain what these changes are and take a closer look at the capital gains tax concessions enjoyed by owners of furnished holiday lets.

Paying Tax at 10%

The coalition agreement between the Conservatives and Liberal Democrats promised to tax capital gains more heavily but with "generous exemptions for entrepreneurial business activities".

The "generous exemptions" came in the shape of a big increase in the lifetime limit for Entrepreneurs' Relief in the June 2010 Budget. The relief was then significantly increased once again in the March 2011 Budget.

Entrepreneurs' Relief currently lets you pay just 10% tax on up to £10 million of capital gains.

Entrepreneurs' Relief can be claimed when you sell or transfer a business. Unfortunately, most rental properties and second homes do not qualify for this relief.

There are, however, two important exceptions:

- Furnished holiday lets
- Your business trading premises

So, if you own furnished holiday lets, or if you have a trading business and own your own business premises, you may be able to pay capital gains tax at 10%.

Entrepreneurs' Relief is covered in greater detail in Chapter 20.

Other Capital Gains Tax Reliefs

So far, the new Coalition Government has not made any changes to any of the other CGT reliefs, some of which are extremely valuable, including:

- Principal private residence (PPR) relief
- Private letting relief
- Holdover relief
- Rollover relief

The value of these reliefs has been greatly enhanced by the increase in the CGT rate and any planning measures that use them will be even more worthwhile than before.

Before the March 2011 Budget there were fears that one of the most valuable PPR rules would be done away with: the one that allows you to elect to treat a second home as your tax-free main residence.

This tax break came under the media microscope recently when it was found that a number of MPs had used it to avoid paying CGT on properties that had been paid for by taxpayers.

Although very few of us have much sympathy for MPs and their tax bills, it is good news for all the other second home owners out there that this tax-saving strategy still works! (See Chapter 8 for more details.)

Converting Income into Capital Gains

The reason why capital gains tax rates were increased was to satisfy the Liberal Democrats' desire to tax capital gains "at the same rates as income so that all the money you make is taxed in the same way".

In particular, the Government wanted to crack down on people converting heavily taxed income into leniently taxed capital gains.

Many investors and business owners will be delighted to know that the changes failed miserably to achieve this result.

In Chapter 19 we take a detailed look at how you can convert income taxed at 40% or more into capital gains taxed at just 18% or 28%.

Worse to Come?

Property investments are mostly long-term investments, i.e. investors hold on to their properties for five or ten years and often much longer.

On the other hand, politicians can and do change tax laws at the drop of a hat.

This puts property investors in a difficult position. If you buy a property today you have absolutely no idea how much capital gains tax you will pay when you eventually sell it.

The effective rate of tax you pay could vary from 0% to 40% or more, depending on the political leanings of the Government of the day and the health of the nation's finances.

Always remember this crucial fact before you take the plunge and buy any property based on current tax rates and reliefs.

Scope of this Guide

The aim of this guide is to give you a thorough grounding in property capital gains tax.

It does not, of course, cover **every** eventuality. So please bear in mind the general nature of the information.

Furthermore, the guide does not cover the capital gains tax rules that applied to property sales before 23rd June 2010.

Individual circumstances vary so it's also always vital to obtain professional advice before you do anything that may have tax consequences.

After reading this guide, however, we are confident that you will have a firm grasp of how capital gains tax is calculated and what you can do to pay less of it when you sell your properties.

As for jargon, there isn't very much of it, you'll be pleased to hear.

We sometimes refer to capital gains tax as just CGT. You may also see us talk about the 'taxman' when referring to HM Revenue & Customs, also known as HMRC.

Tax is all about tax years and some of the examples have dates in them. The UK is one of the few remaining countries that insist on having a tax year that does not run from January to December. Our tax year runs from 6th April in one year to 5th April the next year.

Chapter 2

Just How Bad Is Capital Gains Tax?

The top capital gains tax rate was increased significantly in the 2010 Budget but the tax burden can be mitigated through the many exemptions and reliefs that are still available.

For starters, £10,600 of annual capital gains are tax free. Couples enjoy one capital gains tax exemption each so they can have £21,200 of tax-free capital gains.

Whatever's left over will be taxed at 18% (basic-rate taxpayers) or 28% (higher-rate taxpayers).

Sample Tax Rates

Let's say you and your spouse or partner are both higher-rate taxpayers and sell a jointly-owned property, making a £25,000 profit.

The first £21,200 will be covered by your two annual exemptions and the remaining £3,800 will be taxed at 28%, producing a tax bill of just £1,064.

What this means is that your actual effective tax rate is just 4%:

Profit	Tax	Tax Rate
£25,000	£1,064	4%

Clearly, earning £25,000 of capital gains is a lot better than earning an extra £25,000 of income, especially if you're paying 40% or more in income tax. 40% tax on £25,000 would produce a £10,000 tax bill!

Here are some more examples of effective capital gains tax rates for married couples and others who own property jointly.

These effective tax rates are calculated by deducting two annual exemptions and taxing the remaining profits at 28%:

Profit	Tax	Tax Rate
£50,000	£8,064	16%
£100,000	£22,064	22%
£250,000	£64,064	26%

Clearly, paying tax at 16%, 22% or 26% is quite attractive compared with the tax you would have to pay on an equivalent amount of income.

However, £22,000 or £64,000 is still a lot of tax, but the good news is there are lots of things you can do to reduce your capital gains tax bill... as we'll see shortly.

Chapter 3

How Capital Gains Tax Is Calculated

Before we look at strategies you can follow to reduce your capital gains tax bill, it's important to explain exactly how the tax is calculated under the current rules.

CGT can be extremely complex... but it can also be extremely simple.

To show you how it's calculated, we're going to look at a property investor called Kate who sells a buy-to-let flat.

We'll keep tax terminology and jargon to the bare minimum for now because it gets in the way of understanding how capital gains tax is calculated.

Let's say Kate bought the flat for £200,000 and sold it for £250,000. So she has made a 'profit' of £50,000.

However, she probably doesn't have to pay tax on the whole £50,000 because this is not her true net profit.

She will probably have racked up some costs when she sold the property, such as solicitor fees, estate agent fees and advertising. She will also have paid some costs when she originally bought the property, for example survey fees, stamp duty and more solicitor fees.

These direct costs of buying and selling the property can be deducted when calculating her capital gains tax.

Let's say her total selling costs are £3,000 and her buying costs were also £3,000. Her net gain is now calculated as follows:

	£
Sales proceeds	250,000
Less: Purchase price	200,000
Less: Selling costs	3,000
Less: Purchase costs	3,000
Net Gain	**44,000**

The net gain calculated after deducting these allowable costs is often known as the chargeable gain.

The final thing we have to do to calculate Kate's taxable gain is deduct her annual capital gains tax exemption:

Taxable gain = £44,000 - £10,600 = £33,400

What Tax Rate?

Lastly, we calculate Kate's capital gains tax bill by multiplying her taxable gain by the correct tax rate: either 18% or 28% or a combination of both.

Which rate we use depends on how much income she has:

Higher-Rate Taxpayer

If Kate has total income (e.g. rental profits, salary, or interest) of more than £42,475 in the current 2012/13 tax year, she will be a higher-rate taxpayer. This means her entire taxable gain will be taxed at 28%:

£33,400 x 28% = £9,352

Basic-Rate Taxpayer

If Kate's income is less than £42,475, she will be a basic-rate taxpayer and some or all of her gain will be taxed at 18%.

For example, if she has income of £30,000, this means £12,475 of her basic-rate band will still be available (£42,475 - £30,000).

Consequently, the first £12,475 of her capital gain will be taxed at 18% and the rest at 28%:

£12,475 x 18% = £2,246
£20,925 x 28% = £5,859
Total tax   £8,105

If Kate has no taxable income for the year, or has income of less than her personal allowance (£8,105 for 2012/13), her entire taxable gain will be covered by her basic-rate tax band and be taxed at 18%:

$$£33,400 \times 18\% = £6,012$$

In summary, Kate made a £44,000 net profit selling her flat and will be left with a CGT bill ranging from £6,012 to £9,352, depending on how much income she has earned during the tax year.

Unlike the previous CGT rules – where everyone paid a flat rate of 18% – how much CGT you pay once more depends upon how much income you have earned.

How Much Can Be Taxed at 18%?

The maximum amount of capital gains that you can have taxed at 18% during the current tax year is £34,370. This is the basic-rate tax band for the current tax year which started on 6th April 2012 and ends on 5th April 2013.

However, most people do have taxable income that uses up at least some of their basic-rate tax band. Only those whose taxable incomes are less than the £8,105 tax-free personal allowance – and are therefore not using any of their basic-rate tax bands – can have £34,370 of capital gains taxed at 18%.

Reducing Your Taxable Income

As we shall see in Chapter 10, if you can lower your taxable income during the tax year in which you sell assets like investment properties, you could save significant amounts of capital gains tax.

For the current tax year, the maximum tax saving for a couple who manage to free up two basic-rate tax bands, and have their gains taxed at 18% instead of 28%, is £6,874:

$$£34,370 \times 2 \times 10\% = £6,874$$

Similar savings can be enjoyed every tax year but it is important to note that the basic-rate tax band is currently falling in value.

As most readers will be aware, the Government plans to increase the income tax personal allowance to £10,000. However, to prevent higher-rate taxpayers from benefiting, the basic-rate tax band will be reduced.

For example, in the next 2013/14 tax year, the income tax personal allowance will be increased from £8,105 to £9,205 BUT the basic-rate band will be reduced from £34,370 to £32,245.

Not only does this mean that more of your income could be taxed at 40% instead of 20%, it may also result in more of your capital gains being taxed at 28% instead of 18%.

The Size of Your Capital Gains Also Matters

Remember, it's not just the amount of income you earn that determines your capital gains tax rate. Your capital gains are added to your income, so even someone with no income could pay capital gains tax at 28%.

For example, let's say your taxable gains for the current tax year are £50,000 and you do not have any taxable income.

Your capital gains tax bill will be calculated as follows:

$$£34,370 \times 18\% = £6,187$$
$$£15,630 \times 28\% = £4,376$$

Total Tax   £10,563

Keeping Good Documentation

Before moving on it's important to make one small point about documentation.

When you come to sell a property it's important to have evidence of all your purchase costs, proving how much you spent on legal fees, stamp duty and so on. If you bought the property many years ago this is often easier said than done.

That's why it's imperative, whenever you buy a property, to keep hold of all the documentation showing your various purchase costs.

One easy solution is to always keep a separate ring file that contains all the important documentation for every property you own. File your purchase receipts in there and you should be able to dig them out 10 or even 20 years later!

Improvements

Apart from her buying and selling costs, Kate can also claim a tax deduction for any improvements she made to the property. Why? Because if your property goes up in value by £5,000 after you spend £5,000 improving it, you haven't really made a profit and therefore shouldn't be taxed.

So for every £1 you spend on improvements you can reduce your taxable gain by £1.

Let's say Kate spent £5,000 on some improvements to the property, such as installing an en-suite bathroom in one of the bedrooms. If Kate is a higher-rate taxpayer her CGT calculation will look like this:

	£
Sales proceeds	250,000
Less: Purchase price	200,000
Less: Selling costs	3,000
Less: Purchase costs	3,000
Less: Improvements	5,000
Less: CGT exemption	10,600
Taxable gain	28,400
Tax @ 28%	7,952

So, by remembering to claim her improvement costs, Kate has cut her tax bill by £1,400.

So what exactly are improvements? They're often confused with repairs, which are treated completely differently. We'll return to this issue in Chapter 16.

Summary

That, believe it or not, is as complicated as many property capital gains tax calculations get.

You simply take your basic profit, which is found by subtracting the purchase price from the selling price.

You then deduct your:

- Buying costs
- Selling costs
- Improvements
- Annual capital gains tax exemption

Finally, whatever's left is your taxable profit.

Multiply by 18% or 28% and you have your tax bill.

Some Extra Buying and Selling Costs

We mentioned that some of the costs you can deduct include:

- Solicitors' fees – buying and selling
- Estate agent fees
- Stamp duty
- Survey fees
- Advertising
- Improvements

Another cost you can deduct for capital gains tax purposes is any money you spent defending your property from legal attack. A good example would be legal fees as a result of a boundary dispute.

Apart from your actual improvements you can also deduct any professional fees you incur to obtain planning permission for them.

A Quick Point about Mortgages

A lot of property investors make the mistake of thinking their outstanding mortgage can be deducted when calculating capital gains tax. Mortgages have absolutely nothing to do with capital gains tax and shouldn't feature anywhere in your calculation.

Of course mortgage interest for buy-to-let properties can be claimed as an *income tax* deduction when you do your annual income tax return. But that's entirely separate from capital gains tax.

Proceeds and Base Cost

To keep things simple in Kate's case, we simply subtracted all of her buying and selling costs and improvements.

The formal tax calculation that you see in some textbooks and manuals is a bit different. Under this more formal method, your expenses are separated into two different groups.

Your selling costs are subtracted from the sale price of the property. This gives us your 'proceeds'.

The buying costs and improvement costs are added to the original purchase price of the property. This gives us your 'base cost'.

Your gain is then calculated by subtracting your base cost from your proceeds:

$$Gain = Proceeds - Base\ cost$$

As before, you then subtract your annual CGT exemption and whatever's left is taxed at 18% or 28%.

The result is exactly the same as before but you may need to know what your proceeds and base cost are when reading literature from the Revenue and Customs website or communicating with your accountant.

Chapter 4

Paying Capital Gains Tax & Completing Your Return

Paying Your Tax

We now know how much capital gains tax Kate has to pay – the question is, when does she have to pay it?

Let's say she sold the property on 6th April 2012, i.e. at the very start of the new tax year.

Kate then has to pay her tax by 31st January 2014, the deadline for submitting online tax returns for the current tax year.

This means that Kate can hold onto the taxman's money for 665 days! Unlike income tax, you don't have to pay instalments of capital gains tax throughout the year.

Now, there is a saying in the tax advice business that the next best thing to avoiding tax altogether is deferring it.

By selling a property at the start of the tax year you can enjoy free use of the taxman's money for one year and nine months.

What You Have to Report to the Taxman

In the vast majority of cases, you will have to tell the taxman about any property you sold when you fill in your tax return.

However, there are a couple of exceptions. Firstly, you don't have to report capital gains on your tax return if there's no tax to pay and your total sale proceeds in the year are less than four times the annual CGT exemption:

$$4 \times £10,600 = £42,400$$

So if you sold a property for less than £42,400 and your profit is tax free because it's covered by the annual exemption, you may not have to report it on your tax return.

Of course, there aren't many properties that sell for so little. It's mainly share investors who can take advantage of this concession.

However, if you're part of a group or syndicate of investors who own a property, then you could find yourself in this favourable position.

You also don't have to report sales of property that are fully covered by your principal private residence exemption. In other words, most times when you sell your home, you don't have to tell the taxman about it.

Having said all that, the vast majority of property investors have to report their sales on their tax returns. You do this by completing what's known as the *Capital Gains Summary*. This form can usually be downloaded by typing "sa108.pdf" into a search engine or from this web address:

http://www.hmrc.gov.uk/forms/sa108.pdf

Make sure the form you download has the correct dates for the tax year in question. Alternatively, you can obtain the form by calling the HMRC helpline: 0845 9000 404.

Unfortunately, you cannot just submit a Capital Gains Summary on its own, so you will also have to complete any other parts of the tax return which are relevant to you in the same tax year – even if you do not usually have to submit a tax return.

Chapter 5

Capital Gains Tax - The Big 7

The example with Kate is about as simple as it gets. We'll take a look at some of the complexities that arise shortly.

First of all it's important to spend a couple of minutes discussing the 'Big Seven'. These are seven basic but very important facts about capital gains tax that every property investor should know. Most of them are subject to the occasional exception, but our seven basic rules apply in the vast majority of cases.

Rule #1
Only UK Residents Pay Capital Gains Tax

Most people living in the UK fall into the capital gains tax net. However, you do not usually have to pay capital gains tax if you are non-resident. So if you want to escape capital gains tax altogether all you have to do is emigrate. We'll take a look at the emigration rules in Chapter 17.

Rule #2
Only Individuals Pay Capital Gains Tax

If you use a company to invest in property, it will not pay capital gains tax when a property is sold. Companies pay *corporation* tax on their capital gains. Company capital gains are also calculated differently to those of individuals. Chapter 14 compares the tax treatment of capital gains earned by companies and individuals.

Rule #3
It Doesn't Matter <u>How Long</u> You Own the Property

Before taper relief was abolished it did matter how long you owned the property. The longer you owned it, the less tax you paid. Not any more. Everyone pays capital gains tax at the same rates: 18% or 28%. It doesn't matter whether you have owned the property for one year or 20 years.

Rule #4
All Types of Property Are Taxed the Same Way
... with Two Exceptions!

When it comes to property capital gains tax, it generally doesn't matter what *type* of property you own – the capital gains tax treatment is the same for:

- Buy-to-let flats and houses
- Holiday homes
- Commercial shops, offices, and warehouses

A few years ago many commercial properties qualified for business asset taper relief and this entitled them to a special 10% capital gains tax rate.

This relief has been scrapped and commercial property investors now pay the same capital gains tax as residential property investors.

So if you own a buy-to-let flat in Manchester your capital gains tax will be calculated in exactly the same way as someone who owns an office block in Canary Wharf.

The Exceptions

There are, however, two important exceptions that you will see mentioned time and time again in any discussion of property capital gains tax:

- Furnished holiday lets
- The trading premises **of your own business**

If you own a furnished holiday let (generally speaking, a property that is rented out for no more than 31 days at a time) or if you are a business owner and own the premises out of which you trade, you are entitled to a number of capital gains tax reliefs that no other property investor can enjoy, including:

- Entrepreneurs' Relief
- Rollover Relief, and
- Holdover Relief

These reliefs are discussed in Chapters 20 and 21. For now, the important point to remember is that all property investments are taxed in exactly the same way, with the exception of furnished holiday lets and your own business trading premises.

Rule #5
How You Use the Property is What Matters

A property can be used in lots of different ways. How you use it determines whether capital gains tax is payable when you sell.

For example, you may buy the property to:

• Keep as your main residence	No capital gains tax
• Use in your business	Capital gains tax
• Use as a 2nd home	Capital gains tax
• Rent out ('buy to let')	Capital gains tax
• Develop for profit	Income tax & NI*
• Sell on for a profit	Income tax & NI*

* National Insurance

Generally speaking, the only time you can escape tax altogether is when the property is your main residence. If you own property for any other purpose, your profits will be taxed.

The question then is, do you have to pay income tax (and national insurance) or capital gains tax?

Of course there is a significant difference between the two tax regimes. Income tax and national insurance is levied at up to 52% (falling to 47% from April 2013); capital gains tax is levied at up to 28%.

The other advantage of paying CGT is the annual exemption, which shelters £10,600 of your profits from the taxman.

As a general rule, if you buy a property with the intention of renovating or developing it and selling it for a profit, you are a trader and your profits are subject to income tax and national insurance.

The same applies if you are a speculator, for example if you buy a property at a good price and your dominant reason for buying it was to sell at a profit.

However, if you buy a property to rent out or to use as a second home you will be subject to capital gains tax.

There are plenty of grey areas and in practice you may have more than one objective when you buy a property. Properties can also be used for more than one purpose.

Let's look at an example.

Example

Let's say Anne bought an old farmhouse. She lived in the property for three months and then moved out while substantial renovation work took place. After the work was completed, she rented out the property for six months. Halfway through the period of the lease she put the property on the market and sold it.

This is what one would call 'borderline'. Anne has had some personal use out of the property and has let it out, but she has also developed it and sold it after only a short period of ownership.

This case would warrant a much closer look at all of the circumstances. It should be decided on the basis of Anne's intentions but who, apart from Anne herself, would ever know what these truly were?

Such a case could go either way. The more Anne can do to demonstrate that her intention had been to hold the property as a long-term investment, the better her chances of claiming capital gains tax treatment.

Her personal and financial circumstances will be crucial. For example, if she had got married around the time of the sale, or had got into unexpected financial difficulties, which had forced her to make the sale, then she might successfully argue for capital gains tax treatment.

Rule #6
It Doesn't Matter **Where** You Invest

This has always been the rule but it's worth emphasising because many people in the UK own overseas properties.

UK capital gains tax applies to all your investment properties, whether they are in the UK or abroad.

Some overseas countries have their own capital gains tax, others do not – it doesn't really matter as far as the UK taxman is concerned. You still fall into the UK capital gains tax net.

We see a lot of brochures advertising overseas property investments. Some say things like "No Capital Gains Tax". Remember that is **overseas** capital gains tax they are talking about. You still have to pay UK capital gains tax when you sell.

However, you don't have to worry about paying tax twice. The general rule is that any tax you pay overseas is allowed as a credit against your UK capital gains tax bill.

Rule #7
The Size of Your Income & Capital Gains Matters

Under the old CGT rules that applied before 23rd June 2010, everyone paid tax at 18% – it didn't matter how much income you earned or how big your capital gains were.

Nowadays if you sell a property, your taxable gain will be added to your income. Once your basic-rate tax band has been used up, your capital gains will be taxed at 28%.

This has important implications for capital gains tax planning:

- Family members with low incomes should generally hold properties.

- Consider spreading asset sales over several tax years to utilise more than one basic-rate tax band if possible.

- You should try to dispose of assets during years in which your income is unusually low, for example when you retire.

Summary – The Big 7

Let's just summarise these rules again because they are very important:

- If you are UK resident or ordinarily resident you fall into the UK capital gains tax net. You can avoid UK capital gains tax by emigrating.

- Only *individuals* pay capital gains tax. Companies pay corporation tax on their capital gains.

- It doesn't matter how long you hold on to a property – the tax rates are the same whether it's one year or one decade.

- All property profits are taxed in some way, unless the property is your main residence.

- You will pay income tax if you are actively developing or trading any type of property.

- Most other properties are subject to capital gains tax, including buy to lets, holiday homes, shops and offices.

- Capital gains tax is the same for all these properties... with two exceptions: furnished holiday lets and the trading premises of your own business.

- Furnished holiday lets and business trading premises qualify for some special CGT reliefs: including Entrepreneurs' Relief, Rollover Relief, and Holdover Relief.

- Overseas properties are no exception – they still fall into the UK tax net.

- The size of your income and capital gains could determine whether you pay capital gains tax at 18% or 28%.

Chapter 6

More Complex Issues and Jargon

Not all capital gains tax calculations are as simple as Kate's buy-to-let flat. In this chapter, we are going to look at some of the nitty-gritty rules you may also need to be aware of.

They don't apply to all property sales but, where they do apply, they're important.

The Date of the Sale

Let's kick off with dates. Establishing the exact date of a property sale can be important. For example, you may have to work out whether a sale falls into the current tax year or a later year.

For capital gains tax purposes, the sale is treated as taking place as soon as there is an **unconditional contract**. It's important to note that this may be earlier than the completion date of the sale.

For example, let's say James completes the sale of an investment property on 8th April 2013. James thinks he only has to pay capital gains tax by 31st January 2015.

However, let's say the unconditional sale contract was signed on 1st April 2013 – in other words, just before the end of the previous tax year. The capital gains tax due will be payable by 31st January 2014 – 12 months earlier than he originally hoped.

So, as you can see, establishing the exact date of sale can be important for tax purposes.

Sales to Friends and Family

You should also be aware that sometimes the actual selling price of the property is not used to calculate your capital gains tax.

Why? Because people sometimes try to give property for nothing to close family and friends to escape capital gains tax ... or sell property for much less than it's worth.

If a property is sold for much less than it is worth, there will be little or no profit and therefore no capital gains tax to pay. That's the theory anyway. Unfortunately the taxman doesn't always see it that way.

The legal term for transactions between close family and associates is:

'Not at arm's length'

There are two types of property sales of this nature that the taxman is on the look out for:

Type 1 – Connected Persons

The first is sales or gifts to 'connected persons'. Connected persons include most of your close family:

- Husbands, wives and civil partners
- Mothers, fathers
- Grandparents, great grandparents and so on
- Sons, daughters, grandchildren, great grandchildren etc
- Brothers or sisters
- In-laws
- Business partners
- Any company you or any of the above people control
- A trust where any of the above are beneficiaries

Sales or gifts between 'connected' persons are treated as taking place at the **full open market value of the property**.

So even if you sell a £1 million property to your brother for just £1 you will still have to pay capital gains tax as if you had sold it for £1 million.

You have to be very careful when you give away properties that are sitting on big profits. You will still have to pay capital gains tax but, because there are no sales proceeds, you may not have any cash to pay the tax bill.

In fact, cash is often the best asset to give away because this very rarely results in a CGT bill (sterling has always been exempt and foreign currency bank accounts are exempt from 6th April 2012). Failing that, you should try to give away assets that haven't appreciated much in value.

Type 2 – Other Sales Not at Arm's Length

Apart from sales to close family, there are other sales that are also not at arm's length. The result is the same as before – open market value is used instead of the actual sales price. Examples include:

- Transfers between unmarried partners
- Sales of properties to your employees
- A sale that is part of a larger transaction or a series of transactions

Point 3 may look a little confusing but what the taxman is trying to prevent is people selling assets for less than they're worth and getting some other type of indirect kickback or payment.

Burden of Proof

There's an important difference between these sales and sales between connected family members.

Where sales take place between connected family members it is **automatically assumed** that the transaction is not at arm's length and market value is substituted for the actual sales price.

Where the transaction is not between connected persons, it is up to Revenue and Customs to prove that the sale is not at arm's length – there is no automatic assumption that this is the case.

In reality, of course, it can be difficult for the taxman to prove whether properties are sold for less than they are worth. If you give your house to your common law partner for nothing, it's clear this is a transaction not at arm's length. But if you sell the property for only slightly less than it might have fetched on the open market, it would be more difficult for the taxman to establish that this was not a sale at arm's length.

The only way to truly establish what a property is worth is to sell it on the open market. Failing that, you have to get it valued and valuations can easily differ by 10% or even 20%.

Sales Not for Cash

Sometimes people sell property and instead of getting cash they may get paid with other assets. In these cases, to calculate your CGT, you take the market value of the assets you have been given.

Example

Let's take an extremely simple example. Let's say you sell your holiday home in exchange for stock market shares worth £150,000.

When you come to do your capital gains tax calculation for the property, your proceeds will be the market value of the quoted shares you've been given, namely £150,000.

The Cost of Your Property

Usually the cost figure used in your capital gains tax calculation is the amount you paid for the property. However, there are a couple of special situations where the cost is determined using something else.

Inherited Properties

If you inherit a property and later sell it, the cost used in the CGT calculation is the market value at the date of the previous owner's death:

Capital gain = Sales price – Market value at death

For example, let's say a father died and left his son a property that was valued at £150,000 for probate purposes. The son sells the property for £200,000.

The capital gain is calculated as follows:

Capital gain = £200,000 - £150,000 = £50,000

The son only pays tax on the increase in the value of the property since he has owned it.

Properties Acquired From Spouses

If a married person gives their spouse or civil partner a property, there is no capital gains tax. However, when the transferee spouse eventually sells the property, they have to use the transferor spouse's base cost.

For example, let's say Fiona gives her husband, Alan, a property worth £200,000 which she bought for £100,000. Because they're married, there's no capital gains tax payable at this stage.

Alan later sells the property for £300,000. His capital gain is the price he sold it for minus what Fiona originally paid for it:

Capital gain = £300,000 - £100,000 = £200,000

Note that, if a married couple (or civil partners) separate, the CGT exemption for transfers between them only lasts until the next 5th April after the date of separation (or the date their divorce is finalised, if this is sooner).

Properties Bought Before 1st April 1982

Another case where you don't use the actual cost of the property in the CGT calculation is where the property was acquired before 1st April 1982.

So this one's for those readers who have been in the property game for a long time!

For these properties you have to use the market value on 31st March 1982. Many surveyors are well accustomed to providing 'March 1982' valuations, but this is becoming more of a hypothetical exercise as time goes by.

Summary

We've reached the end of this section, which explains some of the special cases you have to watch out for when calculating capital gains tax.

In summary:

- Your sale takes place as soon as there is a binding contract. This is the date used in your CGT calculation. It is not necessarily the completion date of the sale.

- If you sell or give a property to a connected person (usually close family) you have to pay tax on the full open market value.

- There are other sales not at arm's length you should watch out for (eg, sales to relationship partners).

- If someone pays you in kind instead of in cash, to calculate your CGT you use the market value of the assets you have been given.

- If you sell a property you inherited, use the probate value of the property as your cost.

- If your spouse gives you a property there is no CGT payable. However, when you eventually sell the property, use your spouse's original cost when calculating your CGT.

- If you acquired a property before 1st April 1982, you must use its 'March 1982' value in place of cost in your CGT calculation.

Next, we're going to discuss the main residence exemption, which protects you from the taxman when you sell your home.

Chapter 7

The Principal Private Residence Exemption

When you sell your home the profit is tax free – most of us know that.

Not many people realise just how far this tax loophole can be pushed. For example, it can be used, not just by homeowners, but by property investors as well.

The formal name for this tax relief is the Principal Private Residence exemption, also known as PPR.

Climbing the Property Ladder

Because profits from the sale of your home are completely tax free, it usually makes sense to keep climbing the property ladder during your working life, buying bigger and better homes to live in.

One day you can sell up and downsize. Alternatively, you may wish to retire to a cheaper part of the country. By replacing your expensive home with a cheaper one you can get your hands on a cash lump sum that is completely tax free.

Many people do this to boost their pension savings.

Some DIY enthusiasts use the main residence tax shelter much more aggressively than this. What they do is buy a property in need of repair and live in it for a couple of years while they do it up. They then sell up and move on to the next project. The profit they make from doing up the property will usually be completely tax free.

Some would argue that doing up a house and selling it for a healthy profit is a lot more lucrative than, say, taking a part-time job.

Renting Out Your Old Home

The principal private residence exemption can also be used by buy-to-let investors to earn tax-free profits.

This is because there is a special PPR rule that applies to all properties that have been your main residence at some time during your ownership.

What this rule says is that the last three years you own the property are always exempt from CGT. And it doesn't matter how you use the property during those last three years.

In other words, you can move out of your home, rent it out for three years, and still not pay a penny in capital gains tax. (You will still need to pay income tax on any rental profits though.)

As long as you've lived in the property as your main residence at some point in the past (and during your ownership), you qualify for this tax break.

Example 1

Naz buys a flat in Docklands and makes it his home. He then buys a new home in Mayfair and decides to rent out the Docklands flat. Three years later he sells the Docklands flat for a £50,000 profit.

In this example, the profit is completely tax free – the property qualifies for the principal private residence exemption because it used to be his home and he sold it within three years of moving out.

Here's another example of how this rule can be put to good use:

Example 2

Neil lives in a block of flats. He buys a second flat in the block as an investment. Now he has two choices. He can either rent out the new flat or move into it and rent out the old flat.

Let's say he decides to stay where he is and rent out the new property. Three years later he sells it and makes a £100,000 profit.

His capital gains tax bill could be as much as £28,000:

$$£100,000 \times 28\% = £28,000$$

Let's say he decides instead to move into the new property and rent out his old flat. What will the capital gains tax bill be when he sells the old flat in three years' time?

Because this property used to be his main residence, the last three years of ownership are completely tax free, so Neil's capital gains tax bill is zero!

What this proves is that old homes are much better tax shelters than ordinary buy-to-let properties. It's a mouth-watering tax break and one that should be made use of whenever the opportunity arises.

Calculating Your PPR

So how do you calculate your principal private residence exemption when you do your tax return? It's quite simple and best illustrated with an example.

Let's say Dave has a net gain on a buy-to-let property of £100,000.

He has owned the property for 10 years. He lived in it for one year and rented it out for the rest.

How much is tax free?

Thanks to the final three years rule he gets four years of PPR – the one year he lived in it plus the three bonus years. This means that four out of 10 years are tax free. In other words, 40% of his profits are tax free.

His PPR exemption is:

$$£100,000 \times 40\% = £40,000$$

On a technical note, it's worth pointing out that the £100,000 profit is his net profit after deducting all of his buying and selling costs and improvements.

In practice, all capital gains tax calculations must be carried out more accurately, in *days* rather than years, but the results are much the same.

Private Letting Relief

Let's say you decide to hold on to your old home for more than three years. The final three years will still be tax free but the additional years may be taxable.

However, there's another capital gains tax relief that comes to the rescue in these situations called Private Letting Relief.

To get private letting relief there are two conditions which must be satisfied during your ownership. The property must have been:

- Your main residence at some time, and
- Rented out as private residential accommodation at some time.

It's essential that you rented out the property. A property that has simply been left vacant won't qualify.

How Much is Private Letting Relief Worth?

The absolute maximum you can get is a tax deduction of £40,000. In other words, £40,000 of your profits will escape capital gains tax.

However, if you sell more than one property in the same tax year, you're allowed £40,000 for each and every property.

As long as the property is a former main residence that you rented out, it qualifies for this tax relief.

It gets even better than this. Each owner of the property qualifies for this relief. So a couple may be able to shelter up to £80,000 of their profits per property from the taxman.

Calculating Your Private Letting Relief

The exact amount of private letting relief you qualify for is calculated by looking at three numbers:

1. Your PPR exemption for the property
2. The capital gain made while the property was let out
3. £40,000

Your deduction is the **smallest** of these three numbers.

Point 1 is simple – we've just showed how to calculate the PPR exemption. Point 3 is also simple – it's just a number!

Point 2 is essentially the net profit made while you were renting out the property. For example, if you own a property for 10 years and rent it out for the first five, then this number will be half your gain from the property.

The only quirk you have to watch out for is that this number cannot include the last three years. Why? Because those last three years are covered by your PPR exemption anyway.

It's important to remember that we use the smallest of the three numbers when calculating your private letting relief.

Case Study

Let's briefly run through an example that shows how easy capital gains tax calculations can be, even if you introduce extra reliefs like the principal private residence exemption (PPR) and private letting relief and also to show you how powerful these reliefs can be in helping you pay less capital gains tax.

Let's say Amanda bought a house in Peckham for £200,000. She spent £19,000 improving it and lived in it for just one year. She then received a big promotion and pay rise and decided to move to Notting Hill. She decided to keep the Peckham house and rent it out. Six years later Amanda sells it for £400,000.

So how much tax does she pay? She has doubled her money but is worried there will be a big capital gains tax bill because she only lived in the property for one out of the seven years she owned it.

Assuming her buying and selling costs were £3,000 each, her capital gains tax calculation goes like this:

	£
	£
Sales proceeds	400,000
Less: Purchase price	200,000
Less: Selling costs	3,000
Less: Purchase costs	3,000
Less: Improvements	19,000
Net gain	**175,000**

The next step is calculating the various reliefs Amanda is entitled to. She lived in the property as her main residence so she qualifies for the PPR exemption. She lived there for just one year but remember she also gets the last three years. So, in total, four out of the seven years are tax free.

To calculate her PPR, we simply multiply her net gain by 4/7

$$4/7 \times £175,000 = £100,000$$

This figure is her PPR exemption, which she can deduct from her net gain.

Next, we calculate her private letting relief. We know she has lived in the property *and* rented it out, so she does qualify for this relief. It's the smallest of these three numbers:

- Her PPR exemption – £100,000
- Her gain during the letting period
- £40,000

How do we calculate her gain during the letting period? Well, we know her total gain is £175,000 and we know the property was rented out for six out of the seven years she owned it.

However, we don't count the last three years because that overlaps with her PPR exemption. So, in this case, the gain during the letting period is calculated as follows:

$$£175,000 \times 3/7 = £75,000$$

But, it's the smallest of the three numbers that we use so, in this case, Amanda can claim £40,000 in private letting relief.

Finally, she can deduct her annual capital gains tax exemption and whatever's left over is taxed at 28% (we assume that she is a higher-rate taxpayer).

In summary, Amanda's capital gains tax calculation looks like this:

	£
Sales proceeds	400,000
Less:	
Purchase price	200,000
Selling costs	3,000
Purchase costs	3,000
Improvements	19,000
Net gain	**175,000**
Less:	
PPR 4/7 x £175,000	100,000
Private letting relief	40,000
Annual CGT exemption	10,600
Taxable gain	24,400
Tax @ 28%	**6,832**

Having to pay £6,832 in tax is not a bad result when you consider that she made a profit of £175,000 on the property. Her effective tax rate is just 4%!

Remember the PPR exemption and private letting relief can only be claimed when a property has been your main residence at some time during your ownership.

Before we move on, it's important to answer some of the most frequently asked questions about main residences and tax.

What is Your Main Residence?

This is an important issue, especially if you have more than one home. Your main residence is tax free but what exactly is your main residence?

- For starters, only one property can be your main residence at any point in time.

- That property can be located anywhere in the world – it doesn't necessarily have to be in the UK.

- To qualify for the PPR exemption, the property must usually have been physically occupied as your home. In other words, if you never live in the property, it generally can't be your main residence, even if it's the only property you own.

- You don't have to live in the property permanently, however. Your occupation can be occasional and short, which is why a holiday home can sometimes qualify as your main residence.

- Of course you can only have one main residence at a time so if you decide it's to be your holiday home in, say, Spain, then your house in the UK will no longer qualify and will no longer be completely tax free.

- You can rent out a holiday home some of the time and still claim it as your primary residence... there will, however, be a reduction in the amount of PPR relief available.

- If you have more than one home you can choose which one is your main residence but you must follow a special procedure to do this. More on this later.

- Finally, a property doesn't have to be conventional bricks and mortar – caravans, houseboats, etc, may all qualify for the PPR exemption.

What about Couples?

Each unmarried individual can have one main residence.

This means an unmarried couple can have two tax-free main residences – one each.

Of course, the other requirements still stand – meaning each property must be lived in by the owner.

Married couples, however, can only have one main residence covered by the principal private residence exemption. The same goes for civil partnerships.

If a married couple own two private residences they then have to decide which one is the main residence.

How Long Do You Have to Live in the Property?

This is a question we get asked all the time at Taxcafe.

How long do you have to live in a property so that it qualifies for the principal private residence exemption?

There is no 'hard and fast' rule. What we usually say is that it's the **quality** of occupation that counts, not the length of time. It's recommended that you:

- Move into the property for a substantial period.

- Ensure that all relevant institutions (banks, utilities, Revenue & Customs, etc) are notified.

- Inform your family and friends.

- Furnish the property for permanent occupation.

- Register on the electoral roll at that address.

- Do not advertise the property for sale or rent until after the expiry of a substantial period.

Naturally, some of this advice needs to be adapted slightly where you are adopting a second home as your main residence. (We will look at how to do this in the next chapter.)

It is not possible to provide a definitive view of what would be a 'substantial period'. What matters is that the property genuinely becomes your 'permanent home' for a period.

As a rough guide only, you should plan your affairs on the basis that you will be residing in the property for at least a year but preferably two. Where you are looking to use the principal private residence exemption, you must occupy that property completely wholeheartedly – a mere 'sham' occupation will not suffice.

What if I'm Away from Home Temporarily?

Your PPR exemption remains intact during certain periods of absence from the property. These include:

- Up to 3 years – regardless of the reason
- Up to 4 years – if you're working elsewhere in the UK
- No limit – if you're working abroad.

As regards point 1, the three-year period can be made up of either one period or lots of short periods.

As regards, the second two points, it doesn't matter whether it's you or your spouse who has to work away from home.

However, to protect your PPR exemption, make sure that you:

- Occupy the property as your main residence both before and after you are absent from the property, and

- Do not own any other property that could be treated as your main residence.

What if a Relative Lives in the Property?

A common question is whether you can claim the PPR exemption for a dependent relative who lives in a property you own. Only in limited circumstances is this possible – most notably, the property must have been occupied by your relative before 6th April 1988.

In a nutshell, most people cannot claim this exemption.

What Happens if I Rent Out Part of My Home?

If you take on one lodger it is generally accepted that this will not harm your PPR exemption. A lodger is someone who has their own room but otherwise shares the house.

If you rent out part of your house under other circumstances it is likely to reduce your PPR exemption. However, as long as there are no permanent alterations to the structure of the property, you will probably still get quite a lot of relief.

Example

Let's say you divided your two-storey house into two flats – you lived in the lower half and rented out the upper half. Before you sold it you converted it back into one house, which you occupied.

Let's say after owning the property for 10 years you sold it and your gain is £200,000.

The gain of £100,000 for the lower half that you lived in is fully covered by your PPR exemption and tax free.

But what about the £100,000 gain on the upper half that was rented out?

Let's say you lived in the whole house for two years before converting it into the two flats. The gain of £100,000 on the upper half is fully covered for the first two years when you lived in it AND, thanks to that special rule, the last three years – a total of five of the 10 years.

So, half of the £100,000 gain on the upper half is tax free – leaving £50,000 taxable.

That's not all, however. You also qualify for private letting relief. We won't go through the calculation in this example but the amount you can claim is £40,000.

This leaves you with a chargeable gain of only £10,000, which would be fully covered by your annual CGT exemption.

Bottom line: there would be no capital gains tax payable!

What if I Use Part of My Home for Business?

This is a common scenario. Many taxpayers use a room in their house to run a business – including their property letting business.

If you do this you can claim lots of income tax deductions each year including a proportion of your council tax, mortgage interest, utilities and so on.

However, you have to be cautious if you do this because if that room is used **exclusively** for business purposes then the PPR exemption is not available for that part of your home.

The way to get around this is to ensure that the room is not used exclusively for business purposes. You should restrict your income tax claim to, say, 99% of the office's running costs. For example you could ensure that the office also doubles up as:

- A guest bedroom
- Storage for personal belongings
- A library

Doing this could save you a lot in future capital gains tax but won't have much effect on your income tax claim.

Something in the Garden

The last PPR issue we'd like to take a look at in this chapter is how you can protect this valuable tax relief if you sell off or develop part of your home.

It's a common scenario: a taxpayer has a large garden so he or she sells off part of it for property development.

There are the right ways to do this and there are other ways, which are very, very wrong!

The Wrong Ways

For example, you should NOT:

- Sell your house first before selling the development plot.
- Fence off the development plot or separate it from the rest of your garden before selling it.
- Use the development plot for any purpose other than your own private residential occupation immediately prior to the sale.
- Allow the development plot to fall into disuse.

Each of these will result in the complete loss of your principal private residence exemption for the development plot. And, furthermore, do not assume that the plot is covered by the principal private residence exemption if the total area of your house and garden exceeds half a hectare.

The Right Ways

The easiest thing to do is simply sell off the land without committing any of the cardinal sins described above. The sale will now enjoy the same principal private residence exemption as applies to your house itself.

The Other 'Right Way'

The only drawback to the simple way is that you do not get to participate in any of the profit on the development of the plot.

But, what if you hang on to the plot and develop it yourself? You could then proceed to move into the new property and adopt it as your main residence, which would be tax free.

Your old house can safely be sold at any time up to three years after the date you move out and still be covered by the principal private residence exemption.

The new house should be fully covered by the principal private residence exemption, as long as you move in within a year of the date that development started.

There are some potential dangers here but the exemption should be available if you genuinely adopt the new house as your new main residence.

If, however, the newly developed property were sold straight away, this would give rise to a development profit, which would be subject to income tax and possibly also national insurance.

Chapter 8

How to Avoid Capital Gains Tax on a Second Home

Lots of people have second homes, either in the UK or overseas. But in most cases only one of your homes is covered by your PPR exemption. The other home falls into the capital gains tax net.

Most people keep the status quo and the house they live in most of the time is also their main residence for tax purposes.

This is not necessarily a good idea, however. Sometimes it pays to have your second home treated as your main residence in order to save capital gains tax.

The good news is you can pick and choose which of your homes is to be treated as your tax-free main residence. How do you do that? Within two years of acquiring a second property you can **elect** to make it your main residence.

Furthermore, this election will apply from the date your second property first became available to you as a private residence – usually from the day you bought it.

Example

Let's say Mark lives in a flat in London that he bought a year ago. He then buys a second home in Wales where he spends many long weekends and holidays.

Just under two years later, he realises that his Welsh house has gone up in value a lot more than his London flat. He therefore elects his Welsh house as his main residence. This election automatically applies from the day that Mark first had two residences so, in effect, the Welsh property is tax free since the day he bought it.

Now let's move forward in time. Three years after making the main residence election Mark sells the Welsh house at a substantial gain. This gain is totally tax free because he has elected that property as his principal private residence.

What about Mark's London flat? This has not been his main residence since the day he purchased the Welsh property, five years ago. Remember, the main residence election applies to the Welsh property from day one.

Although the London flat hasn't been his main residence for the last five years, it was his main residence for one year before that. So, if he sells it now, his final three years of ownership will also be tax free thanks to the special three-year rule.

Let's look at the overall tax position on the two properties:

- Starting with the Welsh house, this is totally tax free because the PPR election covered it from day one.

- And what about the London flat? Mark has owned this property for six years. It was his main residence for the first year and so tax free during that time. After that, the Welsh house became Mark's main residence for the remaining five years. However, the last three of those are also tax free. So four out of six years, or two-thirds, of Mark's gain on his London flat is tax free.

Example Revisited

But Mark could have done better than this.

Once you have a main residence election in place (within the critical two-year time limit) you can change your election at any time. Furthermore, the new election can be backdated by up to two years. Let's return to our example to see how this helps.

As soon as Mark decided that he was going to sell his Welsh house, he made a new main residence election in favour of his London flat and backdated it by two years.

Let's say it then took six months before the sale of the Welsh house was completed.

This means that the Welsh house ceased to be Mark's main residence 2½ years before he sold it.

However, we know that any former main residence is also exempt for the last three years, so the Welsh house is still totally tax-free!

How has this helped? The London flat now gains an extra 2½ years as Mark's main residence.

Let's say Mark then sells the London flat three years later, after he has owned it for a total of nine years. The flat then qualifies as his main residence for 6½ years out of nine (the first year and the last 5½).

If Mark had not bothered to change his main residence election and had left things as they stood, his London flat would only have qualified for exemption for four out of the nine years.

The rule is this:

If you have two or more residences and expect to sell your main residence within a year, you should make a backdated election in favour of one of your other residences.

But remember, you can only do this if you made your original main residence election within that critical two-year period.

Which Property Should You Elect?

The important point to remember is that it's not necessarily your most valuable property that should be your main residence for tax purposes – it's the property that is rising in value the fastest.

For example, let's say you have two properties:

- A house in the city worth £400,000, rising in value by £15,000 per year.

- A cottage in the country worth £150,000 but rising in value by £30,000 per year.

Clearly you should elect to treat the cottage as your main residence even though it's not your most valuable property. Why? Because it's generating more profit than the city house and those profits will be taxed unless you make the election.

The great thing about the main residence election is you don't have to gamble – you can wait almost two years to see which property has risen in value the most and choose that property as your main residence.

It's also important to remember that once you make a main residence election you're not stuck with it – it can be changed at any time and you can backdate those changes by up to two years.

In fact, you can apply this strategy to as many properties as you like. For example, if you're lucky enough to have five holiday homes, you can elect to make any one of them your main residence at any time.

And remember all of these properties will then be tax free for the last three years you own them.

Why You Should Always Make an Election

Many people with a second home find that their main home is in fact the most valuable **and** is also increasing in value the fastest. At first glance, it seems obvious that the main home should then remain your main residence for capital gains tax purposes.

However, there are two very important reasons why you should still make a main residence election when you acquire a second home:

- Firstly, making an election within two years of buying your second home preserves your right to change the election later on. So if it ever begins to look like you would prefer your second home to be your main residence, you will still have that option.

- Secondly, a main residence election in favour of your second home can be quickly changed to your main home. Revenue and Customs' own manuals say you can make this change just one week later.

So, if you do this you sacrifice just one week of exemption on your main home but your second home gains three things:

- Main residence status for one week

- More importantly, main residence exemption for the last three years of your ownership

- Finally, you will also get private letting relief if you ever subsequently rent it out. Remember this relief is only available if the property has been your main residence.

So that's three years of exemption and possibly up to another £40,000 of relief in exchange for losing just one week of exemption on your main home.

That's why the rule is: always, **always, <u>always</u>** make a main residence election when you buy a second home.

How Do You Make a Main Residence Election?

Making a main residence election is simple. The election must be made in writing, addressed to 'Her Majesty's Inspector of Taxes' and sent to your tax office.

An unmarried individual must sign the election personally for it to be effective. A married couple or civil partnership must both sign the election.

There is no particular prescribed form for the election, although the following example wording would be suitable for inclusion:

"In accordance with section 222(5) Taxation of Chargeable Gains Act 1992, [I/we] hereby nominate [Property] as [my/our] main residence with effect from [Date]."

Unmarried Couples – Two Main Residences

Whilst married couples enjoy a lot of other tax benefits, unmarried couples are in a more fortunate position when it comes to second homes.

This is because they can have two 'main residences', each qualifying for the principal private residence exemption. This means they can have two properties that are completely free from capital gains tax.

Example

Dean and Geri are unmarried and live together in Manchester in a house that they bought together as joint tenants. They also decide to buy a cottage in the Lake District.

Their accountant advises them to do as follows:

- Geri transfers her share of the Manchester house into Dean's sole name. There's no capital gains tax because this is her principal private residence.

- Geri buys the Lake District cottage in her sole name. This is now the only private residence she owns, so it should be regarded as her main residence and tax free.

- Each partner then makes a main residence election in favour of the property they own.

   This is an important precautionary measure because there is a slight chance the taxman might argue that each partner has an equitable stake in the other person's property. Making the elections puts the question of which property is each person's main residence beyond any doubt.

Establishing the Property as a Residence

The next thing Geri has to do is ensure that the second home does become her private residence.

Actual physical occupation of the property on a habitual basis is essential. Spending one weekend per month in the property, for example, should generally be sufficient.

This regular private use of the property would need to continue for a reasonable period. What is 'reasonable' depends on the facts of the case. Generally, we would recommend at least two years, although, where circumstances do genuinely prevent this, a shorter period might sometimes be acceptable.

More important than the amount of time is the 'quality' of the taxpayer's occupation of the property. This, for example, would include furnishing the property to a sufficient standard to make it a comfortable home.

It's also important not to advertise the property for sale or rent until the 'reasonable' period discussed above has expired.

Once the property ceases to be used by the owner as a private residence, it will cease to be treated as their main residence for capital gains tax purposes. Nevertheless, the principal private residence exemption will generally continue to cover the last three years of ownership of the property.

Renting Out Your Holiday Home

Generally speaking, the property cannot be regarded as a private residence when it is being used exclusively for some other purpose.

If you rent the property out under a formal lease, it will cease to be your private residence immediately. This is because the property will cease to be available to you as a private residence and the required 'habitual' occupation will no longer be possible.

Where the property is rented out for short periods, but not enough to prevent it from being regarded as the owner's home, then the principal private residence exemption may continue but will be restricted by reference to the rental periods.

This brings us to the question of whether you can rent out your second home as holiday accommodation and still benefit from the principal private residence exemption.

Here we come back to the issue of your 'quality' of occupation. If the property is rented out to such an extent that your own enjoyment of the property is hindered to the point where it can no longer be regarded as a 'home', then you will lose the benefit of private residence status on the property from that point onwards.

Tax Tip – Foreign Properties

A second home located abroad can be treated as one partner's main residence for capital gains tax purposes under exactly the same principles as outlined above.

Under the right circumstances, this provides scope to have a capital gains tax-free foreign holiday home!

Do watch out for foreign taxes though!

Wealth Warning

Where an unmarried couple hold property for their private use in a different proportion to the funds they provided, there is a risk of income tax charges under the 'pre-owned asset regime'.

These charges may also apply where one partner transfers a property, or a share of a property, to the other as a gift, or sells it at below market value, and continues to occupy it (as Geri did in our example above).

Such charges can easily be avoided by making an election to have the transferred property or donated funds included in the transferor's estate for inheritance tax purposes. There are some complex issues to be considered here however, so professional advice is needed as usual.

Summary

So far, we've looked at how capital gains tax is calculated, how you complete your tax return, how you can make the most of the principal private residence tax break, including how you can make the most of the 'three year rule', how you can use elections to protect your holiday home from tax and how unmarried couples can have more than one principal private residence.

Now we're going to take a look at a variety of other important capital gains tax planning issues.

This information should help you save extra tax and avoid making costly mistakes.

Chapter 9

Trading vs Investment

The first issue we should address is whether you are in fact subject to capital gains tax in the first place.

This revolves around whether you are a 'property trader' or 'property investor'.

Property trading includes activities like property refurbishment and development and property dealing.

If you are a property trader, you pay income tax and national insurance on your profits and if you are an investor you pay capital gains tax.

The following is a brief summary of the most important tax benefits and drawbacks of each type of property business.

Tax Benefits of Property Investment Businesses

- The best thing about being a property investor is you pay at most 28% capital gains tax on profits from property sales.

- There are also a number of exemptions and reliefs you may be able to claim including:

  - The annual CGT exemption
  - Principal private residence relief, and
  - Private letting relief

Tax Drawbacks of Property Investment Businesses

Being classified as a property investor also has a number of drawbacks. For example, there's very limited scope to offset your rental losses and capital losses. Rental losses can only be offset against rental profits in future tax years but not against your other income, such as your salary. Similarly, capital losses may only be offset against capital gains arising in the same tax year or a future one.

Tax Benefits of Being a Property Trader

The advantages of being taxed as a property trader include:

- Losses can be set off against your other income.

- A property development business can be passed on to your heirs free from inheritance tax when you die.

- It's usually possible to move your business into a company or transfer it to family without any significant tax charges.

Tax Drawbacks of Property Trades

There are some serious drawbacks to being a property trader:

- Your profits are subject to both income tax and national insurance. This means you could end up paying 42% income tax and national insurance and possibly 52% if you earn over £150,000 in 2012/13.

- VAT registration may be compulsory if your annual turnover from certain trading activities exceeds the VAT registration limit (currently £77,000).

Summary – Trading vs Investment

Most people would agree that being taxed as an investor is far more attractive than being taxed as a trader. Investors pay 28% tax at the very most – many traders pay at least 42% tax.

However, you can't choose how you are taxed – it depends on how you act and your intentions.

Nevertheless, there are a couple of things we can say with reasonable certainty.

- If you buy a property and rent it out for several years you are a property investor and will pay capital gains tax when you sell. This is what you want because capital gains tax is usually much lower than income tax. The same goes for second home owners. If you buy a property and use it as a second home for several years you will pay capital gains tax.

- If you buy a property with the intention of doing it up and selling it immediately for a profit, you are a property trader and will have to pay income tax and national insurance.

The Boundary between Investment & Trading

In reality, however, some property investors' intentions are often not clear. If you ask someone what their plans are for their property investments you often hear answers like these:

> "I might sell it, or I might hang on to it for a while if I can't get a good price."

> "We think we'll rent it out for a few years but we might sell if we get a good offer."

> "We'll probably sell a few and rent the rest out."

Naturally, any investor is going to do whatever produces the best result and if an unexpected opportunity comes along they would be foolish not to take it while they can.

For tax purposes though, what we have to do is to establish what the investor's main intention was, at the outset, when the investment was made.

The trouble with intentions, of course, is that they can be very difficult to prove. Who but you can possibly know exactly what was in your mind when you purchased a property?

Looking at it from the taxman's point of view, the only evidence that they sometimes have to go on is the actual facts of what really transpired and this may be very different to what was intended.

Tax Tip

For this reason, it is sensible to document your intentions for your property business.

This could take many forms. Some of the most popular are a business plan, a diary note, a letter to your solicitor or a memo to a business partner.

Remember to date your documentary evidence.

Having something in writing will not necessarily be enough, however. A business plan that says "we will rent the properties out for five years and then sell them" may not be very convincing if you actually sell all your properties very quickly.

Unless, that is, you sold them because of an unexpected change in circumstances. Acceptable reasons for changing your mind could include:

- An unexpected shortage of funds
- An unexpected and exceptionally good offer
- Relocation due to work, family or other reasons
- Divorce or separation
- Bereavements and inheritance
- Concerns over the property market in a particular location
- Funds are required for an exceptional investment opportunity elsewhere

But Life Isn't Always That Simple

Between the extremes of the long-term investor and short-term trader is the 'grey area' where investment meets trading. It's not always so easy to be sure which side of the line you are on.

It is almost impossible for us to give you a definitive answer to explain exactly when investment becomes trading. Here, however, are some useful guidelines:

Renovation and Conversion Work

Renovation or building work may sometimes indicate that there is a trading motive behind buying the property.

However, if you continue to hold the property for several years after the completion of your building work, it is likely that you still have an investment property that will eventually be subject to capital gains tax.

On the other hand, if you sell the property immediately after completing the work, you may well be regarded as a property developer **unless** your original intention had been to keep the property and rent it out, but some change in circumstances led you to change your mind.

Frequency of Transactions

If you only sell a property once every few years, you are likely to be carrying on a property investment business.

If you make several sales every year, representing a high proportion of your portfolio, you may be a property trader or developer.

Number of Transactions

As well as their frequency, the number of property transactions that you have carried out can be a factor in deciding whether you are trading.

Many people like to buy a house, 'do it up', then sell it and move on. If you do this once then you're probably nothing other than a normal homeowner in the eyes of Revenue & Customs. If you do it every six months for ten years, then somewhere along the way you have probably become a property developer.

Finance Arrangements

Long-term finance arrangements such as mortgages are generally indicative of an investment activity.

Financing your business through short-term arrangements such as bank overdrafts will be more indicative of a development or dealing trade. Short-term finance tends to indicate short-term assets.

Length of Ownership

There is no definitive rule as to how long you must hold a property for it to be an investment rather than potentially trading stock.

Naturally, however, the longer the period that you generally hold your properties, the more likely they are to be accepted as investment properties.

Renting the Properties Out

Renting properties out is usually definitive proof that they are being held as investments and not part of a property trade. Like everything else on this list though, it may not be conclusive on its own.

Living in a Property

Living in the property is another useful way to help prove that your intention was to hold it as a long-term asset. Once again though, this may not be enough if the other facts of the case prove to be contrary to this idea.

'Hands On' Involvement

Being actively involved in the renovation or development of a property makes you look like a property developer. Contracting all of the work out looks more like property investment.

Wealth Warning

Remember that everything we have discussed in this section is merely one factor in determining what kind of property business you have.

Ultimately, it is the overall picture formed by your intentions, your behaviour and your investment pattern that will eventually decide whether you have a property investment business or a property trade.

Mixed Property Businesses

What if your business doesn't fit neatly into investment or trading?

If you have a 'mixed' property business, involving both investment and trading, there is a great danger that any property development or property trading may effectively 'taint' what would otherwise be a property investment business. The taxman may then attempt to deny you capital gains tax treatment on all of your property transactions.

Tax Tip

To avoid this danger, you should take whatever steps you can to separate the businesses.

For example, you could:

- Draw up separate accounts for each business.
- Use a different business name for each activity.
- Report the non-investment activities as a different business in your tax return.
- Consider a different legal ownership structure for the non-investment activities (for example, put them in a company or a partnership with your spouse, partner or adult children).

Chapter 10

How to Reduce Your Income and Pay 18% Capital Gains Tax

Under the previous capital gains tax rules everyone paid the same flat rate of 18%. Under the current CGT rules there are three tax rates:

- 10% where Entrepreneurs' Relief applies
- 18% for other gains made by basic-rate taxpayers
- 28% for other gains made by higher-rate taxpayers

We will look at Entrepreneurs' Relief in Chapter 20.

In all other cases, the amount of capital gains tax you pay will now depend on how much income you have earned during the tax year.

The maximum amount of capital gains that you can have taxed at 18% during the current 2012/13 tax year is £34,370. This is the amount of the basic-rate tax band for 2012/13.

Basic-rate taxpayers pay 10% less capital gains tax than higher-rate taxpayers. This means the basic-rate tax band can save each person up to £3,437 in capital gains tax this year:

£34,370 x 10% = £3,437

This creates some interesting tax-planning opportunities:

Income Planning

If you expect to realise a large capital gain, for example by disposing of a buy-to-let property, you may be able to save quite a lot of tax by making sure the disposal takes place during a tax year in which your taxable income is quite low.

In this respect, company owners can manipulate their incomes more easily than regular employees, sole traders or business partners.

The company itself can keep trading and generating profits but the company owner can make sure that very little of these profits are extracted and taxed in his or her hands.

Example

Richard, a company owner, sells a buy-to-let property, realising a net gain of £50,000 after deducting all buying and selling costs. Deducting his annual CGT exemption of £10,600 leaves a taxable gain of £39,400.

Richard hasn't paid himself any dividends during the current tax year and decides to postpone paying any so that £34,370 of his capital gain will be taxed at 18%. The remaining £5,030 will be taxed at 28%. This simple piece of tax planning has saved Richard £3,437 in capital gains tax.

Note that Richard can still pay himself a tax-free salary of £8,105 to utilise his income tax personal allowance. The income tax personal allowance does not interfere with the capital gains tax calculation. (In practice he may be better off paying himself a slightly smaller salary of £7,605 to avoid national insurance as well.)

Other Income Earners

Other income earners may find it more difficult to control their earnings in this manner.

Regular employees (those who aren't company owners) could consider selling assets during years of unemployment, sabbatical years, or tax years in which they set up a new business.

Sole traders or business partners could consider selling assets during years in which their profits are lower than normal, for example during an economic downturn.

Sole traders and partners should also consider selling assets during tax years in which the business is making healthy profits but also has large tax deductions.

An obvious example would be spending on machinery, equipment and commercial vehicles, which qualifies for 100% tax relief under the annual investment allowance. The maximum amount of spending qualifying for this allowance is £25,000 per year from April 2012.

Example

Melissa is a sole trader and earns profits of £50,000 per year. She draws up accounts to 31st March each year. In March 2013, she spends £25,000 on items for her business that are fully tax deductible. As a result, her taxable profits for 2012/13 are £25,000. The first £8,105 will be tax free; the remaining £16,895 will be taxed at 20%.

In May 2013, shortly after the *next* 2013/14 tax year has started, she sells a buy-to-let property, realising a taxable gain of £15,000, after deducting the annual CGT exemption. If she once again has £50,000 of profits from her business but no tax deductible spending to offset, she will be a higher-rate taxpayer and her entire capital gain will be taxed at 28%.

If she had sold the property during the current 2012/13 tax year, £17,475 of her basic-rate tax band would have been available for capital gains tax purposes (£34,370 - £16,895). As a result, all of her £15,000 taxable capital gain would have been taxed at 18% instead of 28%, saving her £1,500 in tax.

Selling Assets after You Retire

It may be a good idea to sell assets like investment properties after you retire and thus have no earnings.

This tax-planning strategy can be used by everyone: salaried employees, self-employed business owners and company owners.

Example

Rebecca is 60 years old and has recently retired. When she was working, she was a higher-rate taxpayer and would have paid capital gains tax at 28%.

She has accumulated £250,000 in a pension plan and also owns five investment properties with a net gain, after deducting buying and selling costs, of £50,000 per property.

She doesn't want to be a landlord forever and decides to wind down her property business by selling one property per year for the next five years.

Fortunately, the pension rules do not require her to withdraw any money from her personal pension, although she should consider withdrawing just enough to use up her tax-free income tax personal allowance. She can keep the rest of her pension money invested and growing tax free.

(Note that we have assumed in this example that Rebecca either defers her state pension or else is entitled to a state pension of less than her personal allowance each year.)

Withdrawing just a small amount of pension income frees up her basic-rate tax band for capital gains tax purposes.

And selling just one property per year allows her to use her basic-rate tax band and annual CGT exemption five times instead of once.

When she sells the first property during the current 2012/13 tax year her taxable gain will be calculated as follows:

£50,000 - £10,600 = £39,400

Her capital gains tax bill will be calculated as follows:

£34,370 x 18% = £6,187
£5,030   x 28% = £1,408
Total tax   £7,595

This means her effective tax rate on the £50,000 profit is just 15%.

It's impossible to say exactly how much tax she will pay on the remaining four properties because we don't yet know what the basic-rate tax band and annual CGT exemption will be for the next four tax years (all we know is that the basic-rate band will be £32,245 in the next 2013/14 tax year).

So, to keep the example simple, we will base the CGT calculation for the next four tax years on the current 2012/13 tax bands and allowances.

Her total bill on the £250,000 of capital gains from the five properties would then be approximately £38,000.

If Rebecca had still been working and had sold all of the properties in one go, she would have been able to use just one CGT exemption and all of her gains would have been taxed at 28%, producing a tax bill of £67,032.

This strategy – postponing the sales until she has no earnings and selling one property per year – could save Rebecca around £29,000 in capital gains tax.

In summary, it is not always possible to manipulate your taxable income but there are times in life when your income will be lower than normal. This is when you should consider selling assets like investment properties.

Chapter 11

How Your Spouse or Partner Can Help You Pay Less CGT

Many of the potential tax savings you can enjoy by keeping your taxable income low and spreading asset sales over several tax years could potentially be doubled up if the asset is owned by both you and someone else, such as a spouse or relationship partner.

In this section we'll look at the tax benefits of joint ownership. Owning a property jointly with someone could reduce the capital gains tax payable by £6,405 and possibly by as much as £17,605.

However, there are also a number of potential traps and drawbacks.

Tax Benefits of Joint Ownership

Prior to the changes announced in the June 2010 Budget, the maximum capital gains tax saving possible from owning a pure investment property jointly with someone else was just £1,818.

Why? Because having one more owner, such as your spouse or partner, meant another CGT exemption could be used when the property was sold. At the time, this meant an extra £10,100 of gains were tax free:

£10,100 x 18% tax = £1,818 tax saving

Following the emergency Budget on 22nd June 2010, however, joint ownership has become a lot more attractive. There are two reasons why this is the case.

First of all, having an additional person's CGT exemption could save you more money now that the top tax rate has gone up from 18% to 28%:

£10,600 x 28% = £2,968 tax saving

Secondly, because basic-rate taxpayers pay capital gains tax at just 18%, it is possible to own a property jointly with someone who has little or no taxable income and up to £34,370 of the chargeable gain will be taxed at 18% instead of 28%, producing a 10% saving:

$$£34,370 \times 10\% = £3,437$$

In summary, owning a property jointly with your spouse or partner could produce a CGT saving of £6,405 (£2,968 + £3,437).

Additional Tax Savings

If the property has been your spouse or partner's main home in the past, they may also qualify for private letting relief of up to £40,000. This means another £40,000 of gains could be tax free, saving you up to a further £11,200 in capital gains tax.

$$£40,000 \times 28\% \text{ tax} = £11,200$$

Maximum Potential Tax Saving for Couples

The potential saving for a property eligible for private letting relief is £17,605:

CGT Exemption + Basic-rate Band + Private Letting Relief

$$£2,968 + £3,437 + £11,200 = £17,605$$

This is the maximum potential saving to be derived from joint ownership of property unless Entrepreneurs' Relief is available (see Chapter 20 for further details).

Can I Benefit?

Only basic-rate taxpayers (those with total income of less than £42,475 in the current tax year) can have capital gains taxed at 18% and only those with taxable income of just £8,105 or less can enjoy the maximum basic-rate band saving of £3,437.

With one or two notable exceptions (certain stay-at-home parents, for example), the majority of readers and their spouses will probably have taxable income of more than £8,105 and many will be higher-rate taxpayers.

However, as mentioned in the previous chapter, even those who are normally higher-rate taxpayers may be able to benefit from the 18% CGT rate at certain points in time.

Furthermore, all higher-rate taxpayers are entitled to an annual CGT exemption, which could save an additional £2,968 this year and similar amounts every other tax year.

Case Study

Jake owns a property which is showing a net profit of £60,000 after deducting all buying and estimated selling costs. He decides to sell the property and wants to know if he should transfer a share to his wife, Sophie, before putting it on the market.

Neither Jake nor Sophie have any other capital gains, so both CGT exemptions are available. We'll also assume that the property has never been their main residence and is therefore not eligible for private letting relief.

How much of the property, if any, should Jake transfer to Sophie? The answer to this question depends on how much income they earn:

Jake and Sophie are both higher-rate taxpayers

Both basic-rate tax bands have already been used up, so the only tax saving from joint ownership will come from using two CGT exemptions.

Jake has to transfer at least enough of the property so that Sophie has a capital gain of £10,600. This means Jake should transfer at least an 18% share in the property (£10,600/£60,000) to Sophie. Simply transferring a half share would achieve the same capital gains tax outcome.

Potential tax saving: £2,968 (£10,600 x 28%)

Jake is a higher-rate taxpayer, Sophie's income is less than her personal allowance (£8,105)

The couple can benefit from Jake's CGT exemption and Sophie's basic-rate band and CGT exemption.

Jake should transfer at least 75% of the property to Sophie:

$$(£10,600 + £34,370)/£60,000$$

He should not transfer the whole property because that would waste his own CGT exemption.

Potential tax saving: £6,405

Jake is a higher-rate taxpayer, Sophie is a basic-rate taxpayer

The couple can benefit from Jake and Sophie's CGT exemptions and some of Sophie's basic-rate band. If, after deducting her income tax personal allowance, Sophie has taxable income of, say, £25,000; this means £9,370 of her basic-rate tax band is still available (£34,370 - £25,000).

Jake should transfer at least 33% of the property to Sophie:

$$(£10,600 + £9,370)/£60,000$$

Transferring a half share would achieve the same CGT outcome.

Potential tax saving: £3,905

Jake's income is less than his personal allowance (£8,105), Sophie is a higher-rate taxpayer

The couple can benefit from Sophie's CGT exemption and Jake's basic-rate band and CGT exemption.

Jake should transfer around 18% of the property (£10,600/£60,000) to Sophie. He should make sure he retains at least 75% of the property:

$$(£10,600 + £34,370)/£60,000$$

Potential tax saving: £2,968 (£10,600 x 28%)

Jake and Sophie are both basic-rate taxpayers

This is the trickiest situation for calculating the optimum property share to be transferred. The couple can benefit from both CGT exemptions and part of each person's basic-rate band.

Let's say, for example, that Jake and Sophie have total taxable income of £18,105 and £13,105 respectively. After deducting their personal allowances of £8,105, Jake has used up £10,000 of his basic-rate band, leaving £24,370 available (£34,370 - £10,000), and Sophie has used up £5,000, leaving £29,370 available (£34,370 - £5,000).

The two basic-rate bands and two annual CGT exemptions add up to a total of £74,940 (£24,370 + £29,370 + 2 x £10,600). This means that it should be possible to avoid having any of the £60,000 gain taxed at 28%.

Jake can achieve the best result by transferring a share in the property to Sophie somewhere between 42% (£25,030/£60,000) and 67% (£39,970/£60,000).

The figure of £25,030 is the minimum amount of gain which Jake needs to pass over to Sophie so that he avoids paying CGT at 28%. It is derived by deducting his annual CGT exemption and his remaining available basic-rate band from the total gain of £60,000:

$$£60,000 - £24,370 - £10,600 = £25,030$$

The figure of £39,970 is the maximum amount of gain which Sophie can have before she pays CGT at 28%. It is derived by adding together her annual CGT exemption and her remaining available basic-rate band:

$$£10,600 + £29,370 = £39,970$$

By passing a proportion of the gain to Sophie which lies anywhere between these two figures Jake can ensure that neither of them pays CGT at 28%.

Transferring a half share would achieve the same CGT outcome in this particular case, but this will not always be so.

Potential tax saving: £4,411 (£10,600 x 28% + £14,430 x 10%)

Transfers Not Between Spouses or Civil Partners

In the previous case study Jake transferred a share in his property to his wife Sophie.

If Jake and Sophie were NOT married the transfer may not have saved the couple any tax.

Joint ownership between unmarried couples, other family members or friends can save tax BUT it is usually best to split the ownership *before* the property has risen in value, for example when the property is first purchased, rather than close to the date of sale.

This is because transferring a share in a property to someone who isn't your spouse or civil partner will usually be treated like a normal sale for capital gains tax purposes.

Example

Jake owns a property that is showing a net gain of £60,000. The facts are the same as before, except Jake and Sophie are NOT married. How much of the property, if any, should Jake transfer to Sophie prior to the sale?

If Jake is a higher-rate taxpayer and Sophie has income of no more than £8,105, he may be tempted to transfer £44,970 of the gain to Sophie (i.e. 75% of the property), so that her CGT exemption and basic-rate tax band can be utilised:

$$£10,600 + £34,370 = £44,970$$

If Jake does this, however, the transfer to Sophie will be treated like a regular property sale and will be subject to capital gains tax at 28% because Jake is a higher-rate taxpayer.

However, one way Jake and Sophie can save tax if they are not married is by utilising multiple CGT exemptions over more than one tax year.

Multiple CGT Exemptions

Although pre-sale transfers between people who are not married may not work (especially if the transfer and sale take place during the same tax year), this group of individuals can do some constructive long-term tax planning and benefit from multiple CGT exemptions.

This is best illustrated with an example:

Example

Hugo and Annica are in a relationship but are not married. Hugo owns a flat worth £100,000 that he originally purchased for £60,000. So he has a potential capital gain of £40,000.

Hugo doesn't want to sell the property but wants to do some long-term CGT planning.

He transfers 25% of the property to Annica. This is a taxable transfer because the couple are not married, so Hugo will be subject to CGT on £10,000 (25% x £40,000).

Fortunately this amount is fully covered by his annual CGT exemption, so no tax is payable. Hugo has managed to transfer one quarter of the property to Annica tax free.

Ten years later, the property is sold for £150,000. Assuming they are both higher-rate taxpayers, the couple will pay capital gains tax as follows:

	Hugo's 75% £	Annica's 25% £
Sales proceeds	112,500	37,500
Less: Acquisition cost	45,000	25,000
Net gain*	**67,500**	**12,500**
Less: CGT exemption**	14,500	14,500
Chargeable gain	53,000	Nil
Tax @ 28%	14,840	Nil

*   We ignore buying and selling costs to keep the example simple
** An estimate of the CGT exemption in 10 years' time

If Hugo had retained 100% ownership of the property he would have paid an extra £6,300 in capital gains tax.

By transferring some of the property to Annica, the couple have managed to benefit from two additional CGT exemptions: once when the 25% share was transferred to Annica and again when the property was sold, thanks to there being two owners.

Extra points to note:

- If Hugo is not in a rush to sell the property, he might be able to increase his tax savings further by making additional transfers to Annica, in subsequent tax years, to utilise more years' CGT exemptions.

- This tax-saving strategy would also work with adult children or other relatives other than your spouse or civil partner.

- Married couples and civil partners cannot do this sort of planning because transfers between spouses do not trigger a capital gains tax liability.

Tax Traps & Drawbacks of Joint Ownership

It usually pays to own a property jointly, but there are circumstances where this may not produce any tax saving:

One of you has a lot of income or gains

The tax saving strategies outlined in this chapter produce the best results when at least one of the people involved in the property transfer has little or no taxable income and/or little or no other capital gains. This allows full use to be made of basic-rate tax bands and CGT exemptions to avoid capital gains tax.

Before making any property transfers, it is important to ensure that the necessary basic-rate bands and/or CGT exemptions will be available when required, either in the year the transfer is made or when the property is eventually sold. Otherwise, the tax planning will be ineffective.

One of you has capital losses to use up

If you have £20,000 of capital losses from selling some shares in a previous tax year and a £30,600 capital gain from selling a property, you can offset your losses against your gains leaving a net gain of just £10,600 which will be covered by your annual exemption.

In this situation, transferring the property to someone else may be pointless. Before you transfer any assets check whether you have accumulated capital losses from previous tax years.

The costs are prohibitive

Transferring a share in a property from one person to another will involve some conveyancing costs. It is likely that these will vary significantly from one solicitor to another. Some will charge just a couple of hundred pounds, others a four figure sum. This cost has to be weighed against the potential tax savings.

Your lender prohibits it

If the property has a mortgage over it, it is possible the lender will place restrictions on any transfer of a share in the asset to another person.

Your spouse is not entitled to PPR relief on the property

In the case of a property on which you are entitled to PPR relief (and possibly also private letting relief), be very careful about any transfer to a spouse or civil partner. The transferee will only be entitled to these reliefs on their share of any gain if they also occupied the property as their main residence at some point during your ownership.

Tax Planning Checklist

Here are some important planning points if you decide to change the ownership of a property before you sell it to save tax:

- Do the transfer as soon as possible, ideally before the property is put on the market.

- Transfers after there is a sale contract will probably be ineffective.

- The person who receives a share of the property must have proper beneficial ownership. Otherwise the transfer will be invalid for tax purposes.

- Joint ownership does not have to mean equal shares – any allocation is possible.

- Married couples and civil partners can usually transfer shares of a property to each other without any immediate capital gains tax consequences.

- Unmarried couples aren't so lucky. Such transfers are generally treated as if the property share had been sold for its open market value. This could result in a significant CGT bill.

- There are ways to avoid this, for example by making a transfer of property into a trust. This allows you to postpone paying capital gains tax. However, such an arrangement costs money and may not be worthwhile if the capital gains tax savings are small. There are also potential inheritance tax consequences which may need to be considered.

- If the property is your former main residence, make sure that the transferee is also entitled to PPR relief on their share of any gain before you make a transfer.

- Finally, ask yourself are the tax savings worth it? The maximum CGT saving you can achieve by transferring a regular buy-to-let property that you've never lived in is £6,405. From that, you'll also have to deduct legal fees and any other costs.

Saving Other Taxes

Joint ownership of property can result in significant income tax savings as well as capital gains tax savings.

However, for joint ownership to produce income tax savings, two things are necessary:

- You have to own properties that actually produce rental profits – many buy-to-let investors make rental losses.

- One of you must be paying income tax at a lower rate than the other. For example, if one person pays tax at 20% and the other pays tax at 40%.

Other Potential Pitfalls

Property transfers can also lead to other tax issues, including:

- **Inheritance Tax:** gifts or sales at less than market value of property, or shares in property, to anyone other than your spouse or civil partner may have Inheritance Tax consequences. Transfers into trust may even give rise to immediate Inheritance Tax charges, although these can generally be avoided with careful planning.

Conversely, when planned carefully, such transfers can provide a useful mechanism for avoiding Inheritance Tax.

- **Stamp Duty Land Tax:** sales of property, or shares in property, at any price in excess of £125,000 (or £150,000 for non-residential property), to any person, will give rise to Stamp Duty Land Tax liabilities for the transferee.

There is no exemption for spouses or civil partners and any mortgage liabilities assumed by the transferee must be counted as sales proceeds.

- **Income Tax:** where a property, or a share in a property, has been gifted or sold at less than market value to anyone other than your spouse or civil partner, you could be subject to income tax charges in respect of any future personal use of that property.

The charges do not apply where your future use of the property is appropriate to the share which you have retained and they can also be avoided by electing for the transferred property, or share in property, to remain within your estate for inheritance tax purposes.

Chapter 12

Save Tax by Selling Your Property Portfolio Slowly

In Chapter 10, we showed how much capital gains tax can be saved by reducing your taxable income during the tax year in which you sell investment properties. This lets you pay capital gains tax at 18% instead of 28%.

We also showed how you can enjoy these tax savings on every property you own by spreading your property sales over more than one tax year.

Selling one property per year also allows you to use your CGT exemption more than once.

In Chapter 11 we showed how all these tax savings can be doubled by owning properties jointly with your spouse, unmarried partner or other relatives.

In this chapter we pull all these tax-saving strategies together and show how a couple can save over £170,000 in capital gains tax by owning properties jointly, minimising their taxable incomes and spreading their property sales over several tax years.

Case Study

Paul and Carrie have achieved their dream of becoming property millionaires. They have built up a portfolio of 20 properties with total net gains of £1 million. They now want to start selling their properties and enjoy their profits.

We are going to assume that the couple do not need to sell all of their properties immediately. They are happy to sell them off at the rate of one per tax year.

Each property has made a profit of £50,000 and receiving a lump sum of this amount every year is enough to make a significant difference to their lifestyle.

The couple take action to ensure they are basic-rate taxpayers. This means they will pay 18% capital gains tax. As we know from Chapter 10, there are several ways to reduce your taxable income, for example by postponing property sales until you retire and keeping your pension plans fully invested.

We will not be too restrictive on the couple, however. We will assume that they can earn up to £28,075 of income each (including, for example, rental income from their remaining properties). This leaves £14,400 of their basic-rate tax bands available to pay 18% capital gains tax.

To keep things really simple, we will assume that everything remains fixed in the years ahead – the value of the couple's properties, tax rates and allowances, etc. In reality, there will probably be many changes but, as with any form of tax planning, we can only plan on the basis of what we know today. (We do know some of the tax rate changes for 2013/14 but, to be consistent, we will ignore these for the sake of illustration.)

So how much capital gains tax will Paul and Carrie pay? Every time they sell a property they will have to pay £2,592 each in capital gains tax, for a total tax bill of £5,184 per property:

	Paul	Carrie
	£	£
Net Profit	25,000	25,000
Less: Annual CGT exemption	10,600	10,600
Chargeable gain	14,400	14,400
Tax @ 18%	2,592	2,592

The total combined tax bill on all 20 properties is £103,680:

20 properties x £5,184 tax = £103,680 tax

The effective tax rate on the £1 million of capital gains is just 10%:

£103,680/£1 million = 10.4%

How much tax do Paul and Carrie save by keeping their taxable incomes low and spreading their property sales?

If the couple sell all of their properties in a single tax year, their capital gains will be added to their income and taxed at up to 28%, producing a capital gains tax bill of up to £274,064:

£1,000,000 - £21,200 CGT exemptions x 28% = £274,064

So, by selling only one property each year, Paul and Carrie save £170,384 in capital gains tax and get to keep an extra 17% of their property profits.

The tax savings are this large because the couple get to use their annual CGT exemptions an extra 19 times and all of their remaining profits are taxed at 18% instead of 28%.

The aim of this case study is to show that you don't have to resort to complex and expensive tax planning to slash your CGT bill.

You just have to follow these three steps:

- Make sure your taxable income is low, so your gains are taxed at 18% instead of 28%.

- Sell your properties over several years so you can benefit from multiple CGT exemptions and basic-rate bands.

- Own your properties jointly to double up your tax savings.

Small Properties vs Big Properties

It also pays, purely from a tax standpoint, to have lots of small properties rather than one or two big ones.

You can do this either by:

- Buying lower value properties, or
- Investing in syndicates or jointly with other people.

This will allow you to eventually spread your sales over a number of tax years and make maximum use of your basic-rate tax band and annual CGT exemption.

From a non-tax standpoint, this is not necessarily the best strategy, however.

The more properties you have, the more time consuming it is to manage your portfolio.

Furthermore, the more properties you buy and sell, the more costs you will incur (legal fees, etc).

At Taxcafe we always say that you should never let the tax tail wag the investment dog.

In other words, tax should only be one factor you consider when you make investment decisions.

Nevertheless, it is interesting to note that a couple with £60,000 in profits spread equally over three properties can sell one per tax year and avoid paying a single penny in capital gains tax.

However, a couple with £60,000 of profits tied up in just one property could end up paying £10,864 in tax when they sell because they will only be able to use one year's worth of CGT exemptions.

Protecting Your Rental Losses

In the case study we just looked at, Paul and Carrie sold their properties over a number of years to save capital gains tax. Another reason it pays to sell your properties gradually is to save *income tax*.

Many property investors have accumulated rental losses from previous tax years because their mortgage interest and other costs, such as letting agent fees, wear and tear and repairs, have exceeded their rental income.

Over many years, these losses could run to tens of thousands of pounds, especially if you have a big portfolio.

Unfortunately, rental losses generally cannot be offset against your salary or other income to reduce your tax bill.

The taxman does, however, let you save up your losses each year and use them to reduce tax when your properties eventually start producing rental profits.

For a higher-rate taxpayer every £1,000 of rental loss is worth £400 in income tax savings, so they're extremely valuable.

However – and this is the important bit – if you sell ALL your rental properties, these valuable rental losses are lost forever.

Rental losses can only be carried forward as long as you continue to have a property rental business.

If you are selling UK properties the trick is to keep at least one UK rental property – that way you will still have a UK property business and your losses can be preserved.

Example

Let's say that, like Paul and Carrie, you own 20 valuable properties that you decide to sell. Let's also say you've accumulated £100,000 worth of rental losses over many years. We've pulled this figure out of the air. In practice, the number could be bigger or smaller, depending on how big your mortgages are and how much rent the properties have generated over the years.

If you sell all of your properties in one go, your property business will cease to exist and your losses will be lost forever.

If, however, you sell your properties one by one over a number of years, you can use the proceeds to reduce the borrowings on the properties you still own.

As your mortgages go down, your remaining properties will start making bigger and bigger rental profits. Rental profits are taxable but, because you have accumulated losses of £100,000, you can earn £100,000 of rental income tax free.

As a result, if you are a higher-rate taxpayer, you could save up to £40,000 in income tax:

$$£100,000 \times 40\% = £40,000 \text{ tax saving}$$

In summary, if you have accumulated rental losses, you will be literally throwing money away if you sell all of your rental properties.

It is far more efficient to:

- Sell off your properties over a number of tax years.
- Use the sales proceeds to pay down the borrowings on your remaining properties.

Less borrowing means more rental profit. This rental profit will be completely tax free while you use up your accumulated rental losses.

Chapter 13

How to Use Your Children's Main Residence Exemption

As soon as your children reach the age of 18, they are each entitled to their own principal private residence for capital gains tax purposes. This provides enormous potential for either parents or their children to enjoy tax-free capital growth on property occupied by young adult children. Many families use the young adult's university years as an opportunity to cash in on this benefit.

As we already know, a property is not only exempt from capital gains tax while it is being used as the owner's main residence, the last three years of ownership are also exempt.

On top of all this, any property that is the owner's main residence at any time during their ownership, and is also rented out as private residential accommodation, is also eligible for private letting relief of up to £40,000.

Example

Patrick's daughter Joanna is about to start a three-year degree course at Purdey University. Patrick gives Joanna £80,000 as a deposit on a four-bedroom townhouse and acts as guarantor for the loan Joanna needs to make up the rest of the £150,000 purchase price.

Joanna moves into one room in the property and rents out the other three bedrooms to friends, using the rental income to fund her mortgage repayments. The four friends share the same kitchen, dining room and living room, so they effectively live as a single household.

Over the next three years, Joanna's tenants come and go and she moves rooms several times, so that she has used each room at some point. At any given time, Joanna is personally using all the common areas (the kitchen, etc) and one of the bedrooms. In this particular case, this amounts to 60% of the property's total floor space.

After graduating, Joanna moves to London and rents her old house out to different groups of students for another five years, before finally selling the property for £280,000.

Capital Gains Tax

In our example, Joanna has made a capital gain of £130,000 over a period of eight years. For three years, she occupied 60% of the property as her own main residence, giving her exemption for £29,250 of her gain (£130,000 x 3/8 x 60%).

She is also exempt for her last three years of ownership. Because she personally used every room in the house at some time, she does not need to restrict this part of her claim and it therefore amounts to £48,750 (£130,000 x 3/8). Joanna's principal private residence relief therefore totals £78,000.

Joanna can also claim a further £40,000 in private letting relief, bringing her total relief to £118,000 and leaving her with a taxable gain of just £12,000. Hopefully, in eight years' time, this should be covered by her annual exemption (currently £10,600), meaning that Joanna has enjoyed £130,000 of tax-free capital growth.

Joanna did very well here, partly because she personally used every room in the property at some time. Opinion is divided on the exact consequences of not personally using part of the property but the best advice must be to make sure the owner does personally use every room.

This personal use could be quite minor, like storing some personal belongings in the room during vacations, or allowing the owner's visiting parent to use the room whilst the tenant is away.

For a smaller property shared with only one other occupant, there would generally be no restriction on the owner's principal private residence relief for a room not used personally.

Rent-a-Room Relief

Although the focus of this guide is capital gains tax, it is also worth mentioning that for the three years she lived in the property, Joanna would be entitled to claim rent-a-room relief to exempt the first £4,250 of her annual rental income from income tax.

This is because she and her tenants lived as a single household. Sharing a common kitchen and/or dining room is the usual indicator for this.

Rent-a-room relief is effectively optional. If Joanna's rental profits calculated under normal principles (i.e. after deducting mortgage interest, etc) come to less than her total rental income minus £4,250, she would be better off not claiming the relief and using the normal basis instead.

She can make this choice on a year-by-year basis by making the appropriate election within twelve months after the 31st January following the relevant tax year.

Keeping the Wealth

In our example, Patrick gave the deposit money to his daughter but some parents prefer merely to lend it to their child. Whether this is for financial reasons, to be fair to siblings, or for some other reason, the same income tax and capital gains tax savings can still be achieved.

One thing the parent generally should not do, though, is own the property themselves. You can lend money to your child, give it to them, or act as a guarantor on a loan but, with one important exception (see below), the child must own the property to benefit from the principal private residence exemption and private letting relief.

Generally, the best way to maximise the tax benefits of your own child's student accommodation is to simply give them all or part of the purchase price so that they can buy the property themselves, just as Patrick did in our example.

After seven years, the gifted funds will be exempt from inheritance tax, thus producing a fabulous 'triple saving' on your child's student accommodation: capital gains tax, income tax and inheritance tax.

Look at Patrick and Joanna. As a family, they may have saved up to £36,400 in capital gains tax (£130,000 x 28%), £5,100 in income tax (£4,250 x 3 x 40%) and £32,000 in inheritance tax (£80,000 x 40%): a total family tax saving of over £73,000!

All this on top of the additional saving in rent during the child's university years: how's that for first-class degree tax planning!

Using a Trust

These fabulous savings are generally only available when the parents are prepared to put a substantial part of the family's wealth in their children's hands.

Not everyone is comfortable with this and many parents prefer to keep the capital growth in their child's student home for themselves, or at least defer the day that the child gains control of the underlying wealth until they are perhaps a little more mature. This is where a trust comes in handy.

Where a property is occupied as a main residence by the beneficiary of a trust, the trust is entitled to the same amounts of principal private residence relief and private letting relief as that beneficiary would have been entitled to if they had owned the property themselves.

This exemption does not apply where a capital gain on a property has been held over on a transfer into the trust, but this is no problem where the property is purchased by the trust in the first place.

Example

Diana sets up a trust with her daughter Emma as the beneficiary and transfers £150,000 into it, which the trust uses to buy a three-bedroom flat.

Emma occupies one of the bedrooms and the trust rents the others to two of her friends. The three friends have just started a three-year course at Peel University. At the beginning of each new academic year, the friends change rooms so that, by the end of the course, Emma has used each room personally.

After graduating, Emma moves to London and the trust rents the property out to other parties. Seven years later, the trust sells the flat for £250,000, realising a gain of £100,000.

The bedrooms take up 54% of the floorspace so, throughout her time at university, Emma personally occupied a total of 64%:

$$46\% + 1/3 \times 54\% = 64\%$$

The trust is therefore entitled to principal private residence relief as follows:

Period of occupation by beneficiary:
£100,000 x 3/10 x 64%   £19,200

Last three years of ownership:
£100,000 x 3/10   £30,000

Total   £49,200

The trust is also entitled to private letting relief of £40,000, giving total relief of £89,200 and bringing the chargeable gain down to just £10,800.

A trust is generally only entitled to an annual exemption equal to half the amount given to individuals. This may perhaps amount to around £7,000 in ten years' time, leaving a taxable gain of about £3,800. The trust will then pay CGT at 28% on this sum (trusts pay CGT at 28% on all capital gains arising after 22nd June 2010).

Nevertheless, although a small amount of capital gains tax might arise, the family would still have saved up to around £26,936 (£96,200 x 28%).

What happens next depends on exactly how the trust was set up in the first place.

Diana may have kept the 'reversionary interest' in the trust. This would mean that the sale proceeds are passed back to her. Her reversionary interest could even have started as soon as Emma left university if she preferred, although this would leave Diana fully exposed to capital gains tax on any future growth in the value of the property thereafter.

Alternatively, the sale proceeds could continue to be held for Emma's benefit until she reached a set age, or even for life. Some families prefer to keep wealth in trust as long as possible, as this protects the beneficiary from problems such as a bad marriage or bankruptcy.

Income Tax

Typically, the income arising in the trust is automatically passed to the beneficiary. This is known as an 'interest in possession' and is a good way to provide the beneficiary with income during their university years and perhaps later. In this way, the trust income is taxed at the beneficiary's top income tax rate, as part of their income, rather than at the trust tax rate, which is currently 50%, but falls to 45% in April 2013.

Final Warning

Whether you give property directly to your child or use a trust, it is important to avoid any significant personal use of the property yourself (or by your spouse or civil partner), as this can lead to income tax charges. You can stay over for the occasional night or weekend when visiting your child but anything more is risky unless you start paying a full market rent.

If you use a trust where you retain the reversionary interest, you can use the property as you wish after it reverts back to you. You will even be able to claim principal private residence relief if you later adopt the property as your own private residence, provided that the trust did not hold over the gain arising on the transfer back to you.

Inheritance Tax

Using a trust may have inheritance tax consequences and professional advice is essential. However, there is not generally a problem if the parent puts no more than an amount equal to the nil rate band (currently £325,000) into the trust and the trust holds the property for less than ten years. Couples can usually put up to £325,000 each into trust without any adverse inheritance tax consequences.

Even when a trust does hold property for ten years or more, there are often little or no Inheritance Tax charges where the amount originally invested did not exceed the nil rate band.

Chapter 14

Using a Property Company to Pay Less Tax

No discussion of property capital gains tax would be complete without taking a brief look at the pros and cons of setting up your very own property company.

This is a complex subject and Taxcafe has devoted a whole publication to it called *Using a Property Company to Save Tax*.

Straight off it's important to point out that if you decide to transfer your *existing* property portfolio into a company, this will be treated as a disposal and will be subject to both capital gains tax and stamp duty land tax.

That's why it's often better to make **new** property purchases through a company, rather than transfer your existing properties.

So what's the best way to invest in property now – individually or using a company?

Recent Tax Changes

The changes to capital gains tax announced in the June 2010 Budget only apply to individuals.

Companies don't pay capital gains tax – they pay corporation tax – and are completely unaffected by the CGT changes.

There were, however, announcements in the March 2011 and March 2012 Budgets that do affect companies.

The main rate of corporation tax has been reduced from 26% to 24% with effect from 1st April 2012 and will be reduced to 23% from April 2013 and 22% from April 2014.

The main corporation tax rate applies to companies with annual profits over £1.5 million.

The small profits rate of corporation tax was reduced from 21% to 20% in April 2011.

The small profits rate applies to companies with annual profits not exceeding £300,000.

As a result of these changes, company owners will see a significant reduction in their tax bills. The recent, current and future corporation tax rates can be summarised as follows:

| Profits | Year Starting 1st April | | | |
	2011	2012	2013	2014
Up to £300k	20%	20%	20%	20%
£300k to £1.5m	27.5%	25%	23.75%	22.5%
Over £1.5m	26%	24%	23%	22%

These corporation tax rates apply to the company's total profits, including its capital gains.

The rate applying to company profits between £300,000 and £1.5 million is sometimes known as the 'marginal rate'. It only applies to the profits or gains which lie in this band, not to the company's entire profits and gains. The first £300,000 of profits or gains is still subject to the small profits rate.

Once a company's total profits and gains exceed £1.5 million, however, it must pay corporation tax at the main rate on all its profits and gains.

Individuals vs Companies: Tax Rates

Individuals generally pay capital gains tax at either 18% (basic-rate taxpayers) or 28% (higher-rate taxpayers).

Companies with no more than £300,000 of total profits, including their capital gains, pay corporation tax at just 20%.

In other words, if you are a higher-rate taxpayer, you will generally pay tax at a much lower rate on your capital gains by using a company (20% instead of 28%).

If your profits are higher than £300,000, your company will pay more than 20% corporation tax. However, companies will always pay tax at a lower rate than the 28% which is usually payable by higher-rate taxpayers.

Individuals vs Companies: Tax Reliefs

Unlike individuals, companies do not enjoy an annual capital gains tax exemption. The annual CGT exemption is currently worth £10,600 per person, which means it can save a couple up to £5,936 in capital gains tax:

$$£10,600 \times 2 \times 28\% = £5,936$$

However, companies are entitled to one tax relief that individuals no longer receive: indexation relief.

Indexation relief eliminates the purely inflationary element of capital gains. The relief is based on the increase in the retail prices index over the period of the company's ownership of the asset.

Generally speaking, indexation relief is much more valuable than the annual CGT exemption.

If a property goes up by 5% per year, an individual could pay capital gains tax on the full 5%. But a company will only pay tax on the real growth, not the inflationary growth. For example, if inflation averages 3%, the company will only be taxed on the remaining 2%:

$$5\% \text{ growth} - 3\% \text{ inflation} = 2\% \text{ taxable}$$

This is a simplistic example of how indexation relief works but illustrates the point.

Potential Tax Savings

The following example illustrates the potential tax saving from using a company.

Example – Capital Gains Tax

Paul and Ina, both higher-rate taxpayers, own a property that they purchased for £200,000. They sell the property 15 years later for £400,000. Their capital gains tax will be:

	£
Sales proceeds	400,000
Less:	
Purchase price	200,000
Annual CGT exemptions*	33,000
Taxable gain	167,000
Tax @ 28%	**46,760**

* An estimate of two CGT exemptions in 15 years' time

Example – Corporation Tax

Paulina Ltd owns a property that was purchased for £200,000. The company sells the property 15 years later for £400,000. The retail price index rises by 55% over the period (equivalent to inflation of 3% per year). The company's corporation tax on the capital gain is calculated as follows:

	£
Sales proceeds	400,000
Less:	
Purchase price	200,000
Indexation relief	
£200,000 x 55%	110,000
Chargeable gain	90,000
Tax @ 20%	**18,000**

In this example, using a company produces a tax saving of £28,760. Similar savings could be enjoyed every time the company sells a property.

However, as with many examples like this, a different outcome could be pulled out of the hat if the numbers were tweaked enough. It is possible for individuals to pay less tax on their capital gains than companies.

For example, the indexation relief could be smaller than the CGT exemption if the property was very small or if there had been very little inflation. And, if the individual was a basic-rate taxpayer, subject to capital gains tax at just 18%, the tax rate would be lower than the corporation tax rate.

Generally speaking, however, a company will usually pay less tax on its capital gains than an individual, especially if the individual is a higher-rate taxpayer paying 28% capital gains tax.

Loss Relief

Another big tax benefit of using a company to invest in property is that companies can potentially offset their *rental losses* against their *capital gains*.

Why is this valuable? Many investors who have borrowed money in the past decade to buy investment property have accumulated rental losses. In other words, the rents have not been big enough to cover the mortgages and all the other costs.

If you're an individual investor, the problem with these losses is that they cannot be offset against your salary or other non-property income and they cannot be used to reduce your capital gains tax when you sell a property.

You can, however, offset them against your current taxable rental profits. With mortgage interest rates quite low at present, many property investors are starting to make bigger rental profits and these accumulated rental losses will help them save income tax.

Nevertheless, when interest rates do eventually rise again, many investors will return to much lower levels of rental profit once more.

Companies have much more flexibility when it comes to using their accumulated rental losses. A company can offset its rental losses against its capital gains from selling property.

For example, let's say your company sells a property and makes a gain of £20,000. If the company has accumulated £20,000 of rental losses over the years, it won't pay a penny in tax on that capital gain.

Companies and Rental Income

It's not just tax on capital gains that you can save by using a company.

You could also save a fortune in tax on your rental profits.

Companies pay corporation tax on their rental profits, so that means just 20% tax on rental profits of up to £300,000.

Individuals pay income tax on their rental profits, which means tax at rates of up to 40% or 50% (the 50% rate will be reduced to 45% in April 2013).

Using a company could therefore leave you with a lot more after-tax rental income to help you grow your property portfolio.

Getting the Money Out

A company will probably pay less tax on its capital gains and rental income than an individual who is a higher-rate taxpayer.

So what's the catch?

The catch is that, if you use a company to invest in property, you may end up paying *additional tax* when you take money out of the company.

If you pay out your after-tax income or capital gains as a dividend, for example, the dividend will be taxed at the following rates in 2012/13, depending on your income status:

- Basic-rate taxpayers   0%
- Higher-rate taxpayers   25%
- 'Super tax' taxpayers   36.1%

'Super tax' applies to individuals with total taxable income of more than £150,000. It does not affect the rate of capital gains tax paid by the individual, which remains 28%.

The additional tax on dividends received from your property company can be avoided by:

- Only extracting dividends when you are a basic-rate taxpayer (i.e. when they are partly or totally tax free).

- Selling your shares in the company, rather than the properties themselves. The sale of property investment company shares is taxed in exactly the same way as the sale of investment property by an individual.

Long-term Wealth Accumulation

Using a company to invest in property makes most sense when the company is used as a long-term wealth accumulation vehicle.

Low corporation tax rates could leave you with a lot more rental income and capital gains after tax. These extra profits can be reinvested and as a result the property portfolio could grow faster than one owned by an individual.

Money can be extracted at certain opportune times when this will not create a significant additional tax bill, for example when you retire and are a basic-rate taxpayer.

Ultimately, the company and its properties do not even have to be sold. Shares in the company could be left to your children or other heirs who can enjoy the rental income for decades to come.

Non-tax Factors

Finally, remember that tax is just one factor to consider and there are lots of non-tax benefits and drawbacks to using a company.

For example, they can provide significant legal protection because they are separate legal entities.

However, you may find it more difficult to find buy-to-let mortgages for properties owned by a company.

Summary

- Individuals generally pay capital gains tax at 18% or 28%.

- Companies pay 20% tax on the first £300,000 of profits.

- Companies never pay tax on capital gains at a higher rate than the normal CGT rate for higher-rate taxpayer individuals.

- Individuals enjoy an annual CGT exemption

- ... but companies get indexation relief

- ... and can offset their rental losses against their capital gains.

- You may pay additional tax when you extract money from your company

- ... although this additional tax can be avoided.

- ... and there are other non-tax reasons why using a company could be attractive or unattractive.

Chapter 15

Tax Benefits & Dangers of Remortgaging

Getting the ownership structure for your properties right is imperative, and involving your spouse, partner or children, or setting up your own property company, could potentially save you thousands of pounds in tax.

Another thing you have to structure carefully is your borrowings. In recent years a lot of property investors have remortgaged their properties aggressively as a way of getting their hands on their profits without having to sell any properties.

The good news is this money is completely tax free.

For example, let's say you are able to borrow an extra £20,000 by remortgaging a buy-to-let property.

That money can be used as a deposit on another buy-to-let property or you could use it to pay for personal living expenses, children's education, a new car, or a holiday even.

Whatever you decide to do with the money, the whole £20,000 is yours and you don't have to pay any tax on it.

Capital gains tax generally only comes into the picture when there is a property disposal. If you remortgage a property, you haven't made a disposal because you still own it. So there's no capital gains tax to pay.

Income Tax

When you remortgage you will, of course, have to pay interest.

The question is whether that interest is tax deductible.

In most cases, it doesn't matter whether you remortgage your own home or a buy-to-let property. Whether the interest is tax deductible generally depends on one thing and one thing alone – how you **use** the money.

Use it to buy a new investment property and the interest is tax deductible.

If you use the money for personal reasons – to pay for a new car, for example – the interest is generally not tax deductible.

There is an important exception to this rule, however. When you remortgage a rental property up to its value when first introduced into your rental business, your mortgage interest is tax deductible, whatever you spend the money on!

Dangers of Remortgaging

A lot of property investors forget that remortgaging does not reduce your capital gains tax bill, it simply postpones it.

If and when you eventually sell the property, you will have to pay the bank back all the money you borrowed and you will have to pay the taxman all your capital gains tax.

Remember that when you calculate your capital gains tax, you cannot deduct the mortgage over the property. Mortgages have absolutely nothing to do with capital gains tax. They cannot be claimed as an expense.

Remortgaging is a good way of avoiding capital gains tax initially but some property investors have borrowed too aggressively in recent years, leaving no cushion to protect themselves against falling property prices.

If you have remortgaged your properties too aggressively, you may not have enough money at the end of the day to pay back your loans and pay your capital gains tax.

Example

Steve bought a property for £200,000. Over the years it increased in value to £450,000 and Steve remortgaged up to 85%, which is £382,500.

He then decided to sell the property but only managed to get £405,000.

How much is left over for Steve after repaying the bank and the taxman?

We will assume that he is a higher-rate taxpayer and had buying and selling costs of £3,000 each. His capital gains tax calculation looks like this:

Sales proceeds	£405,000
Less: Purchase price	£200,000
Less: Selling costs	£3,000
Less: Purchase costs	£3,000
Less: CGT exemption	£10,600
Taxable gain	£188,400
Tax @ 28%	£52,752

He also had to pay back the bank £382,500, so overall Steve is left with a shortfall of £33,252, calculated as follows:

£405,000 - £3,000 selling costs - £382,500 mortgages - £52,752 tax

= - £33,252

That money will have to come from somewhere else because there isn't enough money from the property sale to cover all the loans and tax.

Escaping the Trap

To avoid this trap, investors have to borrow responsibly, taking account of their future CGT bills.

In theory, with a top capital gains tax rate of 28%, you should never borrow more than the cost of the property plus 72% of any increase in value.

In practice, however, you also need to allow for potential future falls in property values or further increases in CGT rates. It therefore makes sense to reduce this 'maximum borrowing' figure by a further factor to give you a margin of safety. The greater the reduction, the greater your margin of safety: many commentators recommend a further reduction of at least 10%.

If Steve in our example had followed this strategy, he would have limited his borrowing to just £342,000 and he would then have had enough money to repay his mortgage and pay his capital gains tax bill.

If you are planning to sell existing properties that have *already* been aggressively remortgaged, make sure you have enough money not just to pay back the bank but to cover any capital gains tax as well.

Interest vs Capital Gains Tax

Although mortgage brokers love it when you remortgage your properties, we're not convinced it's always the best thing to do.

It's a good idea when the property market is strong and you want to use the money to buy more investment properties.

But when the property market is weak it may be more sensible to keep your borrowings down and reduce the risk in your buy-to-let portfolio.

We're also not convinced that remortgaging is a good idea if you take the money and spend it on personal items such as general living expenses. In these cases, the interest often isn't tax deductible and will soon add up.

For example, let's say you sell a buy-to-let property and your net gain is £25,000 after deducting all your buying and selling costs and improvements. If you own the property jointly with a spouse or partner (and therefore enjoy two CGT exemptions) your capital gains tax bill will be no more than £1,064.

Let's say instead you remortgage the property and, because your existing borrowings are quite low, you are able to borrow an extra £25,000. If the interest rate on your mortgage is, say, 5%, your annual interest cost will be more than your tax bill from selling the property:

$$£25,000 \times 5\% = £1,250$$

More importantly, that interest has to be paid, not just once, like capital gains tax, but every year!

So remortgaging can postpone tax in the short run but it can also be extremely expensive in other ways.

Are we saying that you should sell your properties instead of remortgaging them? Not necessarily. You may have good reasons to hold on to your properties for many years into the future.

However, you should always think twice about remortgaging a property just to get your hands on some cash to spend.

Chapter 16

Improvements vs Repairs

You cannot deduct your mortgages when you calculate CGT but one big cost you can deduct is improvements.

However, a lot of investors don't fully understand the tax difference between repairs and improvements.

Repairs are an income tax deduction and can be claimed every year when you do your tax return.

Improvements can only be claimed when you sell your property and calculate your capital gains tax.

The question is: what is a repair and what is an improvement?

It's a crucial question because repairs can currently give you immediate tax relief at a rate of 40p in the £1 (possibly even 50p or 60p in the £1), whereas improvements can only be claimed when you sell your property and only save you tax at a maximum rate of 28p in the £1.

However, in some situations, improvements could save you more tax than repairs, for example if you have rental losses from previous years. These losses will offset your current rental profits which means you do not have to worry about paying income tax on your rental income. This means obtaining tax relief for repairs will not save you any money at present.

We'll try to provide some answers to the repairs versus improvements question in the pages that follow. However, it's important to stress that deciding what is a repair and what is an improvement can be a complex issue and it is essential to consult a tax professional if significant amounts of money are involved.

Freestanding Items

First of all, it's important to realise that only fitted items that are part of the fabric of your property, such as new windows, fitted kitchens and bathrooms, can be classed as improvements and deducted when you calculate your capital gains tax.

When it comes to freestanding items such as carpets, curtains, electrical goods and appliances, these items can never be claimed as improvements.

For a detailed discussion of the income tax treatment of these items, we would recommend picking up a copy of Taxcafe's guide, *How to Avoid Property Tax*.

Repairs vs Improvements

So what are repairs and improvements? There are two basic principles:

- Spending that **restores** the property to its previous condition is a repair.

- Spending that **enhances** the condition of the property beyond what it used to be is an improvement.

Example 1

Geri has a small townhouse in Kensington which she rents out. She decides to build a conservatory costing £40,000, including £2,000 to redecorate the adjoining room.

Geri's conservatory is an improvement because she is enhancing the condition of the property. So she can only claim the expense when she sells the property and does her CGT calculation.

Redecorating is usually allowed as a repair but in this case it's part of the overall capital expenditure because it's a necessary part of the building work.

Example 2

Emma owns a row of shops that she has been renting out. A massive storm damages the roofs and Emma has these repaired at a cost of £50,000. Emma's cost is a repair cost, which she can claim against her rental income.

It's a repair because she is restoring her property to its previous condition.

Emma Example Continued

The same storm also damaged several windows in Emma's shops. The glazier advises that it will be cheaper to replace the original wooden frames with new PVC double glazing and she agrees to do this. This expenditure is a repair, despite the fact that the new windows represent an improvement on the old ones.

This is because if, due to changes in fashion, or technological advances, it becomes cheaper or more efficient to replace something with a more modern alternative, the fact that it's an improvement can be ignored and the expense can be classed as a repair.

Example 3

Victoria has a flat that she has been renting to students. She decides to upgrade it for the young professional market. Her costs are as follows:

- £16,000 on a new fitted kitchen.

- £3,500 redecorating the bathroom, including £2,000 to replace the existing toilet, sink and bath and £500 to install a shower (there was only a bath before).

- £3,000 repainting the rest of the flat.

- £3,000 on rewiring.

How much is repairs and how much is improvements? Remember the repairs can be claimed as a tax deduction when she fills in her annual tax return. The improvements can be deducted when she sells the property and does her CGT calculation.

The Kitchen

The cost of a new fitted kitchen replacing a broadly similar one would be a repair expense. This would extend to the costs of re-tiling, re-plastering, plumbing, etc.

If Victoria's new kitchen has extra storage or other extra features that weren't present before, then a proportion of the expense will be treated as a capital improvement.

In an extreme case, where fairly standard units are replaced by expensive customised items using much higher quality materials, then the whole cost of the new kitchen will need to be regarded as a capital improvement.

Bathroom

Replacing the existing toilet, basin and sink should usually be a tax-deductible repair.

Once again replacing these existing fittings with expensive customised ones would amount to a capital improvement.

Fitting the new shower will definitely be a capital improvement as this is an item of equipment that was not present before.

The remaining bathroom redecoration costs will need to be apportioned between repairs and improvements. Any expense arising due to the installation of the new shower will be treated as an improvement.

Redecorating the Flat

Most of the redecoration work, in the absence of any building work in the rooms concerned, should be fairly straightforward repairs expenditure.

Rewiring

The rewiring cost will be fully tax deductible as a repair if it is simply 'new for old'. If, on the other hand, Victoria took the opportunity to fit a few new sockets then there will be an improvement element and, as usual, an apportionment would be required.

Newly Acquired Properties

We've already stated that spending that restores the property to its previous condition is a repair.

However, it's important to point out that when we talk about 'previous condition' we're talking about since **you** have owned the property – not before.

So, if you buy a property with a hole in the roof, the cost of repairing the roof will be a capital improvement.

Where both building work and redecoration take place simultaneously in a newly acquired property, it is likely that all of the expenditure will be regarded as a capital improvement.

However, simply modernising the décor in a newly acquired property, when no other work is undertaken, would generally continue to be a repair expense.

The Taxman's View on Newly Acquired Properties

In the case of any expenditure on newly acquired rental properties, Revenue & Customs' own manuals specifically state that any expenditure that is not allowed for income tax purposes on the grounds that it represents capital expenditure should then be allowed for capital gains tax purposes on a disposal of that same property.

Chapter 17

Emigrating to Avoid
Capital Gains Tax

What if you want to completely avoid capital gains tax altogether?

Probably the most drastic thing you can do in that case is to leave the country.

A few years ago it was possible to go and live in certain countries for just one year and completely avoid paying tax on your investment profits.

This was a fantastic loophole, especially when capital gains tax was levied at rates of up to 40%.

Unfortunately that loophole was closed and you now have to live abroad for at least five complete UK tax years to avoid capital gains tax. That's a long time to live away from your friends and family!

For example, let's say you have a portfolio with £150,000 of profits. The maximum tax you will pay is £42,000:

$$£150,000 \times 28\% = £42,000$$

Would you be willing to live overseas for five years to save £42,000 in tax? That's a tax saving of £8,400 per year. Some people would, others wouldn't. Remember, moving abroad is an expensive and time-consuming business and these costs will eat into your tax savings.

What if you have £1 million of profits? In that case, the maximum tax you will pay is £280,000:

$$£1 \text{ million} \times 28\% = £280,000$$

Would you be willing to live overseas for five years to save £280,000 in tax? That's a tax saving of £56,000 per year. Many people would be willing to but, again, some wouldn't.

Of course, if you plan to emigrate one day anyway, this is all academic. You may be able to live in the country of your dreams **and** avoid paying tax at the same time.

However, you have to make sure you sell your assets in the right way because there are significant traps awaiting the unwary.

At present, it is necessary to become non-UK ordinarily resident, as well as non-UK resident.

This is a complex field of tax planning, however the key points worth noting are:

- Emigration must generally be permanent, or at least long-term (usually at least five complete UK tax years).

- You must not sell any assets until non-residence has been achieved.

- Your property sales must be delayed until the tax year <u>after</u> the year you emigrate.

- Limited return visits to the UK are permitted.

- If you return permanently to the UK before five years are up you will have to pay all the capital gains tax.

- Finally, it's essential to make sure you do not end up paying capital gains tax in another country – there's no point in 'jumping out of the frying pan and into the fire!'

Return Visits

As we said, limited return visits to the UK are permitted. At present, the general rules on return visits are:

- They must not exceed 182 days in any one UK tax year.

- They must average less than 91 days per year.

Any day on which you are present in the UK at midnight is counted as part of a return visit for these purposes (unless you are merely in transit from one foreign country to another).

However, it is important to stress that this is only one factor that determines your non-resident status.

At present, Revenue and Customs will look at many other factors, and the more links you maintain with the UK, the more likely you are to continue to be treated as UK resident and liable for capital gains tax.

In the March 2012 Budget, the Government confirmed that it will introduce a more cut and dry 'statutory residence test' from 6th April 2013. This will, hopefully, make it much easier for taxpayers to determine their residence status, without having to rely on case law and vague guidance from HMRC.

Chapter 18

Enterprise Investment Schemes

If you don't want to emigrate and don't want to pay any capital gains tax when you sell your properties, one solution is to reinvest your profits in Enterprise Investment Scheme shares.

These investments let you postpone capital gains tax and help you reduce your income tax.

The investment must take place within three years of selling the property. It can also take place up to a year before you sell the property.

It is even possible to defer capital gains tax by investing in your own trading company!

Unfortunately, however, companies involved in property are generally ineligible to issue Enterprise Investment Scheme shares.

Alternatively, there are products that let you spread your risk when investing in these intrinsically risky investments.

There's no limit on the amount that can be invested in Enterprise Investment Scheme shares if you need to defer a big capital gain.

However, it's important to stress that Enterprise Investment Scheme shares let you **postpone** capital gains tax but do not avoid it altogether. The gain you postpone becomes subject to capital gains tax when those shares are sold.

For the current 2012/13 tax year, qualifying investments of up to £1 million in an unconnected company may also carry an income tax credit of up to 30% of the amount invested. In other words, if you invest £100,000, you could reduce your income tax on your salary or other income by £30,000.

Enterprise Investment Scheme investments may also be carried back for income tax relief in the previous tax year. In effect, by 2013/14, this will mean that a person who did not make any

Enterprise Investment Scheme investments in the previous year will be able to get income tax relief on an investment of up to £2 million.

Combining the income tax credit with the capital gains tax deferral makes these investments extremely powerful tax shelters.

The Seed Enterprise Investment Scheme (SEIS)

This new scheme, introduced with effect from 6th April 2012, provides income tax relief at 50% to individuals investing up to £100,000 per tax year in qualifying companies.

Furthermore, where a capital gain arising in 2012/13 is reinvested in SEIS shares during the same tax year, it will be completely exempted from capital gains tax. This is considerably better than the Enterprise Investment Scheme, where capital gains are only deferred until the shares are sold.

This provides the opportunity to obtain up to 78% tax relief in total – leaving only 22% of the amount invested exposed to the inherent commercial risk of investing in small businesses.

There is a cumulative limit of £150,000 for the total amount raised by a company under the scheme. The scheme is targeted at 'new start-up companies' but this may include an existing company starting up a new trade.

Investors must not be employees, but may be directors. They must not hold, nor be entitled to acquire, an interest of more than 30% in the company's share capital.

There are many, many further restrictions, including the fact that the company must be carrying on a qualifying trade or research and development, so professional advice is essential.

Chapter 19

How to Convert Income into Capital Gains

The reason why capital gains tax rates were increased in the June 2010 Budget was to satisfy the Liberal Democrat Party's desire to tax capital gains "at the same rates as income so that all the money you make is taxed in the same way".

In particular, they wanted to crack down on people converting heavily taxed income into leniently taxed capital gains.

Many property investors and others were delighted to discover, however, that the new capital gains tax rules had failed miserably to achieve this result!

Capital gains, including those made over short periods of time such as one year, are now taxed at no more than 28%, compared with the 40% income tax rate faced by many property investors.

Of course, most property investors pay less than 28% tax on their capital gains thanks to the annual exemption and other CGT reliefs.

For example, a couple of higher-rate taxpayers who enjoy two annual exemptions will face the following effective CGT rates in 2012/13:

Gain	Effective Tax Rate
£20,000	0%
£50,000	16%
£100,000	22%

Clearly, paying 16% tax on a capital gain of £50,000 is much better than paying income tax at 40% or more.

It is hardly surprising, therefore, that some property investors are still actively seeking ways to convert heavily taxed rental income into lightly taxed capital gains.

Is it possible to do this? Yes, but there are two risk areas to consider:

- Tax risk, and
- Market risk

The main tax risk is that capital gains tax could be increased again. Such an increase could include an increase in capital gains tax rates or the withdrawal of special reliefs and exemptions.

As we stated at the very start of this guide, politicians can and do change tax laws at the drop of a hat.

So, as a word of warning, do not assume that the current capital gains tax rates will apply when you come to sell your investments. You should think long and hard about any investment decisions that you will later regret if capital gains tax is increased in the meantime.

The second risk area when it comes to converting income into capital gains is market risk. Here I am talking about the danger that you will lose money and end up converting precious income into capital losses!

Many legitimate techniques for converting income into capital gains involve some market risk.

Two methods you can consider to convert income into capital gains as a property investor include:

- Gearing up your portfolio using borrowed money
- Spending money on 'improvements'

Gearing Up Your Portfolio

This is best illustrated with an example:

Joan has £100,000 and uses it to invest in a single buy-to-let flat. She has no borrowings. The flat produces a rental profit of £5,000 per year. After income tax at 40% she is left with £3,000. Over the next 10 years the flat grows in value by 3% per year and the rental income grows by 3% per year. She reinvests her rental profits and earns 3% per year after tax.

After 10 years the property will be worth £134,000 and her reinvested rental profits will come to £39,000 – total assets £173,000.

Her friend Paul also has £100,000 but uses it to invest in four buy-to-let flats costing £100,000 each. He borrows the extra £300,000. The four flats produce rental income of £20,000 per year but all of it is used to pay mortgage interest (he goes for a long-term fixed rate to reduce risk but the higher rate eats up the rental income on all four properties).

Paul has given up rental income in return for capital growth on a much bigger chunk of property. His mortgage interest is allowed as a tax deduction against his rental income, so he is effectively converting income into capital gains.

The four properties rise in value by 3% per year and are worth a total of around £538,000 after 10 years. He decides to sell three of the properties to pay back his borrowings and get his hands on some cash.

We will assume he structures his affairs so that he earns very little income during the tax year in which the properties are sold, thus freeing up his basic-rate tax band for 18% capital gains tax.

The three properties are worth £403,000 and his profit is £103,000. The capital gains tax bill is calculated as follows:

	£
Net gain*	103,000
Less: CGT exemption**	14,500
Taxable gain	88,500
£40,000*** x 18%	7,200
£48,500 x 28%	13,580
Total tax	**20,780**

* Buying and selling costs ignored for simplicity
** An estimate of the future CGT exemption
*** An estimate of the future basic-rate tax band

After paying his tax bill and paying back his borrowings, Paul is left with £82,220:

	£
Proceeds 3 properties	403,000
Less:	
Capital gains tax	20,780
Borrowings	300,000
Net proceeds	82,220

Paul is left with a single property worth £134,000 (just like Joan) but £82,220 in the bank – total assets £216,220.

In summary, Paul, the heavily geared property investor, ends up with 25% more money than Joan.

What this example shows is that even when property prices are rising very slowly – by just 3% per year – it is possible to boost your returns significantly using gearing and convert heavily taxed rental income into leniently taxed capital gains.

If property prices were to rise by, say, 5% per year, Paul could end up with over 50% more money than Joan.

But what about market risk? It hardly needs spelling out. Joan had no borrowings but Paul was in hock to the tune of £300,000. A 25% drop in property prices would wipe out his investment altogether. A sharp increase in interest rates could become impossible to service out of the properties' rental income.

Spending Money on 'Improvements'

If you spend money on your existing properties, the expense is normally treated as either a repair or an improvement (See Chapter 16 for a detailed discussion).

From a tax-planning perspective, repairs are generally good because they are immediately tax deductible and can save you up to 40% or 50% income tax.

Improvements are generally not so good because tax relief is only provided when the property is sold and will only save, at most, 28% capital gains tax.

Obvious examples of repairs are things like broken windows, leaking roofs, etc. Improvements are generally new features that were not present in the property before and therefore increase its value: extensions, attic conversions, etc.

Between these two extremes, however, is a hybrid type of repair spending that provides income tax relief at 40% to higher-rate taxpayers AND will possibly increase the value of your property.

Spending on this type of repair is therefore a way of converting heavily taxed rental income into leniently taxed capital gains.

Examples of this hybrid type of repair include:

- New kitchens
- New bathrooms
- Double glazing
- Re-wiring
- Most decorating costs.

Many property investors think of these items as improvements but they are in fact fully tax-deductible repairs... provided you follow the rules we outlined in Chapter 16.

To be treated as repairs, it is important that you replace old items with new items and do not add something new that was not present in the property before.

For example, replacing a tatty old kitchen is a tax-deductible repair. If you add *extra* kitchen units or sockets, these additional items will be improvements.

Replacing a pea-green bathroom is a tax-deductible repair. Installing a shower or downstairs toilet where there wasn't one before is an improvement.

Remember, when replacing old items it is also important that you do not substantially upgrade the quality – that would be an improvement.

However, it IS acceptable to install items that are of superior quality when they are simply the nearest modern equivalent. For example, the taxman would not expect you to replace old single glazing with new single glazing when double glazing is the accepted modern standard.

Replacing MDF or similar kitchen units from the 1970s with MDF from 2012 would be a tax-deductible repair. Replacing them with bespoke oak units would be an improvement.

The Risks

Spending money on new kitchens, bathrooms and the like in existing rental properties is arguably a lot less risky than borrowing heavily to invest in new properties.

However, there is no guarantee that such spending will actually increase the value of your properties pound for pound. For example, you may spend £6,000 on a new kitchen, which only increases the property's ultimate selling price by £3,000.

However, done wisely and in the right circumstances, such spending should result in an increase in either the rental income generated by the property, the value of the property, or both.

Chapter 20

Entrepreneurs' Relief

Entrepreneurs' Relief allows each individual to have up to £10 million of capital gains taxed at just 10% instead of 18% or 28%. This can produce tax savings of up to £1,800,000.

Because Entrepreneurs' Relief applies on a *per person* basis, the more people who own the asset (your spouse or partner, children, etc), the more tax you could save!

For example, a couple can enjoy up to £20 million of capital gains taxed at 10%, producing a combined tax saving of up to £3.6 million.

The lifetime limit was raised from £5 million to £10 million with effect from 6th April 2011.

That's the good news. The bad news is that very few property investors can benefit from Entrepreneurs' Relief.

Who Qualifies?

Entrepreneurs' Relief is supposed to benefit those selling *trading* businesses. If you are a buy-to-let investor, the taxman treats you as a business owner, but not as a trading business owner.

Trading businesses are, for want of a better word, "regular" businesses – the likes of shopkeepers, dressmakers, consulting engineers, graphic designers ...and thousands more like them.

Some types of property business are trading businesses, including firms of estate agents, letting agents, chartered surveyors and many property developers.

However, a business loses its trading status when it owns significant investments, including rental properties, and will not receive any Entrepreneurs' Relief.

Property and Entrepreneurs' Relief

Some types of property do, however, qualify for Entrepreneurs' Relief.

Because Entrepreneurs' Relief is available when you sell your trading business, this would include the properties out of which the business operates, i.e. your business premises.

There is one additional type of property that qualifies for Entrepreneurs' Relief: furnished holiday lets.

Furnished holiday lets are specifically mentioned in the Entrepreneurs' Relief legislation and are the one exception to the rule that rental properties do not qualify.

So if you own holiday cottages and apartments, you may be able to pay capital gains tax at just 10%. (See below for the qualifying criteria.)

In summary, the only types of property that can qualify for Entrepreneurs' Relief are:

- The trading premises of *your own business*
- Furnished holiday lets

Trading Premises

Entrepreneurs' Relief can save you a lot of tax when you sell your trading premises, but there are some restrictions and time limits:

- Your property generally only qualifies if you are also selling the business. If you continue trading but sell your trading premises, you will generally not be entitled to any Entrepreneurs' Relief.

- You can qualify for Entrepreneurs' Relief if you sell *part* of the business, but that part must be capable of operating as a going concern in its own right.

- You must have owned the business for at least one year before selling.

- If you simply cease trading instead of selling the business, you can still qualify for Entrepreneurs' Relief on any assets of the business which are sold within three years after the cessation.

What if You Own the Premises Personally?

Lots of businessmen and women who own companies also *personally* own the premises out of which their companies operate.

If you sell your company, any properties that you personally own, but which are used by the company, may qualify for Entrepreneurs' Relief. This is known as an 'associated disposal'.

There are, however, some restrictions. For starters, the company must be a 'personal company', which means:

- You must own at least 5% of the ordinary shares
- Those shares must also give you at least 5% of the voting rights
- The company must be a trading company
- You must be an officer or employee of the company (non-executive directors and company secretaries qualify)

Each of these rules must be satisfied for at least one year before the company is sold or ceases trading.

Furthermore, the property only qualifies for full Entrepreneurs' Relief if there was no rent payment from the business to you for any period after 5th April 2008.

For many business owners this last requirement is the real killer blow and will prevent them from claiming Entrepreneurs' Relief. (The taxman's reasoning is that if the property is only available if rent is paid, it is an investment asset and not a business asset.)

Most people who own their own premises get their companies or business partnerships to pay them rent.

If the rent you receive is the full market rent for the property then you may not be able to claim any Entrepreneurs' Relief when you sell the property.

The Good News

There are two pieces of good news here:

- Any rent received in respect of periods before 6th April 2008 is disregarded.
- Rent paid at less than the market rate only leads to a partial reduction in Entrepreneurs' Relief.

Example

Dick sells his company and the property used by the company (owned personally by Dick) on 5th April 2013.

Dick has owned the property since 5th April 2004 (9 years) and rented it to the company for 100% of the market rent until selling it.

Dick is not entitled to any Entrepreneurs' Relief for the five-year period after April 2008 because he received 100% of the market rent.

Dick is entitled to full Entrepreneurs' Relief for the four-year period before April 2008 because those years do not count.

If the gain on the property is £100,000, Dick's Entrepreneurs' Relief will be reduced as follows:

$$5/9 \times £100,000 = £55,556$$

What this means is that £55,556 of the gain will NOT qualify for Entrepreneurs' Relief and will be taxed at 28%. The remaining £44,444 will qualify and will be taxed at 10%.

If the company had paid Dick just 75% of the market rent, his Entrepreneurs' Relief would have been slightly less restricted:

$$5/9 \times 75\% \times £100,000 = £41,667$$

The remaining £58,333 would qualify and would be taxed at 10%.

If you personally own the property used by your business, it may still make sense to keep paying yourself as much rent as possible (but not more than a market rate), despite the restriction in your Entrepreneurs' Relief. This is because rent is a relatively tax-efficient way of extracting money from your company. Each case therefore needs to be reviewed on its own merits.

Furnished Holiday Lets

Furnished holiday lets qualify for Entrepreneurs' Relief and other capital gains tax and income tax reliefs. These are covered in detail in another Taxcafe guide, *Furnished Holiday Lets*.

The purpose of this section is to give you a brief overview.

The qualifying criteria for furnished holiday letting tax status are quite strict. For the current 2012/13 tax year:

- The property must be situated in the UK or elsewhere in the European Economic Area.
- The property must be furnished.
- It must be let out on a commercial basis with a view to making a profit.
- It must be available for commercial letting for at least 210 days in a 12-month period (140 days in 2011/12).
- It must be actually rented out for at least 105 days (70 days in 2011/12).
- The property must generally not be occupied by the same person for more than 31 consecutive days during a holiday 'season' of at least seven months.

A taxpayer with more than one furnished holiday letting property may use a system of averaging for the 105-day test.

The property does not have to be in a recognised holiday area but must be rented out to holidaymakers and tourists to qualify.

It is clear from the above that merely owning a holiday home in Cornwall or Spain that you rent out occasionally will not necessarily entitle you to the special tax reliefs enjoyed by owners of furnished holiday lets.

Since 2010/11, you may elect to have properties which qualified in the previous tax year treated as furnished holiday lets for up to two further tax years, even if they fail to meet the minimum letting period requirement.

In effect, this means that properties will generally only need to meet the 105-day test once every three years. The property will still need to meet all of the other tests, however, and you will have to make genuine efforts to meet the 105-day test every year.

Using the Property Yourself

Where there is some other use of the property during the year, the capital gains tax reliefs described above will be restricted accordingly.

Nevertheless, it remains possible for the taxpayer and their family to use the property privately as a second home during the 'off season' and still fit within the rules described above.

Selling Individual Properties

In theory, Entrepreneurs' Relief is supposed to be available when *part* of a business is sold, where that part is capable of being run as a going concern in its own right.

If you own more than one furnished holiday let, the question is can you sell just one and qualify for Entrepreneurs' Relief? An individual furnished holiday property should be capable of being run as a going concern in its own right. So a capital gain from the sale of just one property should theoretically qualify for Entrepreneurs' Relief if:

- The property is a furnished holiday let when sold, or

- The property is sold within three years of ceasing to be used as a qualifying furnished holiday let.

However, we are aware that, in practice, HM Revenue and Customs does not agree with this interpretation and may challenge an Entrepreneurs' Relief claim made on the disposal of a single furnished holiday let when the owner retains, and continues to run, other furnished holiday lets.

Sadly, therefore, the correct position is currently unclear and we must await a decisive case in Court before we can be certain!

Summary

- Entrepreneurs' Relief lets individuals pay tax at just 10% on up to £10 million of capital gains.

- This is a lifetime limit.

- Entrepreneurs' Relief applies on a *per person* basis, so couples can have up to £20 million of capital gains taxed at 10%.

- Only two types of property can qualify for Entrepreneurs' Relief:

  ➢ The trading premises of your own business
  ➢ Furnished holiday lets

- Trading premises generally only qualify for Entrepreneurs' Relief if you are also selling your business.

- If you *personally* own the trading premises out of which your personal company operates, the property may still qualify for Entrepreneurs' Relief.

- The Entrepreneurs' Relief will, however, be reduced if the company pays you rent.

- If the company pays you a full market rent, you will not be entitled to any Entrepreneurs' Relief. If you receive half the market rent, your Entrepreneurs' Relief entitlement will be reduced by 50%, and so on.

- Rent paid for periods before 6th April 2008 does not need to be counted for this purpose.

- Furnished holiday lets are properties rented out to holidaymakers for generally no more than 31 days.

- The sale of most furnished holiday lets will qualify for full Entrepreneurs' Relief and 10% capital gains tax. However, it is currently unclear whether the owner has to sell, or cease, the entire business to qualify.

Chapter 21

How to Use Rollover Relief to Postpone Capital Gains Tax

The capital gain from sale of a property used in your own trading business may be rolled over into the purchase of a new trading property.

This effectively defers capital gains tax on the original property until the new property is sold.

The new property can be purchased up to one year before and three years after the original property is sold.

Furnished holiday lets also qualify for this relief.

Full relief is generally available only if the old property was used exclusively for 'trading purposes'.

The entire sale **proceeds** of the old property must be reinvested and not merely the capital gain arising. Any shortfall is deducted from the amount of gain eligible for rollover.

If there is less than full trading use of the property then an appropriate proportion of the gain arising may be rolled over.

Example

Stavros sells an office building in June 2012 for £400,000, realising a capital gain of £100,000.

Stavros has owned the building since June 2002 and, up until June 2007, he rented all of it out to tenants. From June 2007 until the date of sale, however, Stavros used two thirds of the building as his own premises from which he ran a property development trading business.

Stavros is therefore eligible to roll over £33,333 (£100,000 x 5/10 x 2/3) of his capital gain into the purchase of new trading premises.

The eligible amount has been restricted by reference to both the time that the property was used for trading purposes and also the proportion of the property used for trading purposes.

In August 2012, Stavros buys a small gift shop in Cornwall for £120,000 and begins to use it as his own trading premises.

Stavros is therefore able to claim rollover relief of £20,000. He cannot claim the full £33,333 that was eligible for rollover, because he has not reinvested the whole qualifying portion of his sale proceeds (£400,000 x 5/10 x 2/3 = £133,333).

The new qualifying property does not need to be in the same trade or even the same kind of trade. It could even be a furnished holiday let.

There is no minimum period for which the new property needs to be used for trading purposes, although it must be acquired with the intention of using it for trading purposes.

In our example, Stavros could run the gift shop for, say, two years and then convert it into residential property. His capital gains tax rollover relief would not be clawed back, although he would have a reduced base cost for the property when he eventually came to sell it.

Tax Tip

Where you have a capital gain eligible for rollover relief, it is only necessary to use the replacement property for trading purposes for a limited period.

This might include initially running the new property as a guest house or furnished holiday let before later converting to long-term letting, or even adopting it as your own home.

Chapter 22

Deathbed Tax Planning:
How to Completely Avoid CGT

It is said that there are only two certainties in life: death and taxes. However, there is some comfort in the fact that one of these certainties can sometimes be used to reduce the impact of the other.

Sadly, this does not mean that paying more tax will make you live longer (although the Government might try to convince you otherwise), but what it does mean is that death can sometimes be used as an opportunity to save tax.

When we think of death and taxes, we usually think of inheritance tax: and rightly so – because that evil grave robbers' tax is indeed a major problem for many bereaved families. But, as far as capital gains tax is concerned, death can actually provide the means to save tax.

CGT Uplift on Death

When assets pass to another person on death, they may or may not be subject to inheritance tax but they are generally exempt from CGT. Furthermore, not only are they exempt, but the new owner is treated as if they had acquired the asset at its market value at the date of death.

This is what we call the CGT uplift on death and, under the right circumstances, it can provide a major tax-saving opportunity.

What are the 'right circumstances'? Well, the best tax-saving opportunities arise when a member of a married couple or civil partnership dies holding assets such as investment property or stock market investments.

These assets will generally attract capital gains tax at 28% on a sale or lifetime transfer, or inheritance tax at 40% on death, but can usually be passed to a surviving spouse free of both taxes.

Example

Tony and Janet are a married couple and joint owners of a portfolio of investment properties worth £1 million. The properties were purchased many years ago for a total of £200,000.

Ideally, the couple would like to pass the properties to their daughter Jamie but this would give rise to capital gains tax of £224,000.

They have looked into using a trust to pass some of the properties to Jamie but this would only work for the first £650,000 worth of property (without giving rise to an immediate inheritance tax charge) and, even then, both of the couple would need to survive for at least seven years.

They decided against the trust route due to concerns over Tony's health and, indeed, a little while later, his health deteriorates further and his doctors advise that he has only a short time left to live.

Tragic as this is, the family seize their opportunity and Janet transfers her share of the investment properties to Tony before he dies. These transfers are exempt from capital gains tax because they are between spouses.

On his death, Tony leaves everything to Janet, so there is no inheritance tax because all the transfers benefit from the spouse exemption.

Janet is now treated for capital gains tax purposes as if she had purchased the properties for their current market value of £1 million – including her original half share that she transferred to Tony just before he died.

She can now either sell them or transfer them to Jamie but, either way, she should have no capital gains tax to pay.

If Janet does transfer the properties to Jamie, and survives for at least seven years thereafter, there should be no inheritance tax on them either. In fact, some savings would begin to accrue even after just three years.

The interesting thing about this planning is that it is rather counter-intuitive. We are all used to the idea of divesting ourselves of assets as we get older in order to reduce our family's inheritance tax bill. But, as we can see from the example, this family saved £224,000 by transferring assets **to** a dying parent.

Now that we have the transferable nil rate band for inheritance tax purposes, most families will have nothing to lose by using this planning method – and everything to gain!

Exceptions

There are a few exceptions, however. Where one or both of the couple is already a widow or widower (or surviving civil partner) from a previous marriage, there can be more benefit in transferring some assets directly to a child or other beneficiary on death.

The tax-free uplift for capital gains tax still applies, however, so transferring assets to the dying spouse before death will usually still yield savings.

Some care needs to be taken where the family is seeking to pass assets to the next generation quite soon after the first parent's death.

Where there is any type of request, no matter how informal, asking the beneficiary under a will to transfer inherited property to another person and the beneficiary does indeed make the requested transfer within two years of the deceased's death, the transfer is treated as a direct transfer from the deceased to that other person.

In our example above, this would mean that inheritance tax was payable on the properties which Tony left to Janet.

It is all too easy to trigger this provision. Even if the dying Tony simply said to Janet "you will look after Jamie, won't you", HMRC might construe this as an informal request and apply the provision (we have no idea how they sleep at night!).

In short, what happens after the first spouse's death has to be left entirely in the hands of the survivor. If in any doubt, the survivor could avoid the risk posed by this provision by waiting two years and a day after the deceased's death before passing the assets on to the ultimate recipient.

There are two potential drawbacks to this, however.

Firstly, the second spouse would then need to outlive the first by at least nine years for the properties to pass completely free of inheritance tax. Even so, there will be cases where the survivor's life expectancy is long enough to mean that this is not a massive concern and this risk can also be covered through term assurance.

Secondly, the widow or widower would be exposed to capital gains tax on any growth in the value of the properties between the date of the deceased's death and the date of the transfer to the ultimate recipient.

This may mean that the properties cannot be passed on totally tax-free but 28% on two years' growth is certainly a lot better than 40% on the entire value!

In most cases, however, the most difficult thing about this planning may be the fact that the action required has to be carried out at a very stressful and emotional time. Nevertheless, if the Government is hard-hearted enough to use death as an opportunity to raise taxes, why shouldn't we use it as an opportunity to save them?

Pitfalls to Watch Out For

This type of planning will work well for some families but there are a few things to watch out for.

Firstly, where the surviving spouse is non-UK domiciled for inheritance tax purposes, the spouse exemption for inheritance tax is currently capped at just £55,000, so this planning may not work as intended.

Remember also that the spouse exemptions for both capital gains tax and inheritance tax apply to legally married couples and registered civil partners only.

Furthermore, the capital gains tax exemption for transfers between spouses does not apply where the couple have separated before the beginning of the tax year in which the transfer takes place.

Any mortgages or other borrowings over the properties transferred can lead to stamp duty land tax liabilities, or even mean that the transfers cannot take place (we all know how co-operative banks are these days!)

But, most of all, the survivor needs to be sure that the transferred properties will indeed come back to them when their spouse dies. There cannot be any arrangement which guarantees this or the planning would not work: it has to be left to the dying spouse's will.

So, before undertaking this planning, the healthy spouse should ask themselves whether there is any risk that the dying spouse might leave the properties to some mysterious third party, or even just to the local cat and dog home. These things do happen and, whilst the law provides some protection to bereaved dependents, it will seldom extend to investment properties!

Lightning Source UK Ltd.
Milton Keynes UK
UKOW041809180213

206470UK00006B/834/P